ARMENIAN CHRISTOLOGY
AND
EVANGELIZATION
OF ISLAM

ARMENIAN CHRISTOLOGY
AND
EVANGELIZATION
OF ISLAM

A SURVEY
OF THE RELEVANCE OF THE CHRISTOLOGY OF THE ARMENIAN
APOSTOLIC CHURCH TO ARMENIAN RELATIONS WITH ITS MUSLIM
ENVIRONMENT

BY

HAGOP A. CHAKMAKJIAN

A.B., B.D., Th.D.

LEIDEN
E. J. BRILL
1965

PRINTED IN THE NETHERLANDS

TO MY WIFE
MARITZA
AND OUR CHILDREN
VASKEN PAUL, ALICE, SUSAN, HILDA
AFFECTIONATELY AND GRATEFULLY
DEDICATED

TABLE OF CONTENTS

PREFACE

The Near or Middle East, the cradle of Judaism, Christianity, and Islam, has been dominated by Islam for thirteen centuries. Millions of Christians have dwelt in this region as subjects of Muslim rulers. And yet, in spite of this long and continuous contact between Muslims and Christians, there are no organized churches in this area composed of Muslim converts to the Christian faith, excepting a *very* small group in Persia.

This book is a modest attempt to inquire into *one* of the many causes of this failure. While all Christian communions of this region are equally implicated in this failure and ineffectiveness, this writer will speak only of what he has discovered about his own people and their Church—the Armenian Apostolic, as well as Evangelical, Church—leaving the others to their own children to survey.

Originally, this thesis was prepared in 1950–53 as partial requirement for a doctorate at the Pacific School of Religion in Berkeley, California. We are glad to note that during the intervening years the Armenian Apostolic Church has joined the World Council of Churches, thus taking a significant step. However, only future will tell if this nontheological association with the family of churches will also influence her monophysitic position. Since no doctrinal revision has taken place yet in the position of the Armenian Church, the *main* thesis of this dissertation remains unchanged.

The study is based on Armenian history—political as well as ecclesiastical—interpreted in the light of the Christian faith and theology, general and church history, and the history of religion and missions.

This opportunity cannot be passed without expressing my deep gratitude to my three supervising professors of the Pacific School of Religion—Dr. Hugh Vernon White, Chairman; Dr. Georgia Harkness, and Dr. Ralph Hyslop—whose cordial and vigilant surveillance and constructive criticisms and suggestions while the study proceeded have added considerably to the strength of the argument. Likewise, my heartiest thanks are due to President Stuart Anderson and the Faculty of the said School for scholarships granted me which made this research possible.

Also, my cordial thanks are due to my publishers for their courtesy, patience, and cooperation, and to many authors and their publishers of copyrighted materials for generous permission to use the citations duly acknowledged in the text.

Above all, this book is dedicated to my wife and our four children not as a matter of sentimentalism but out of deep gratitude and love. For, unquestionably, without the courage and fortitude of a loyal spouse, my academic endeavors would have been simply impossible—beginning with basic seminary training in the School of Religion in Athens, Greece, and continuing in Beirut (Lebanon), Hartford, Andover-Newton and Harvard, Fresno, and Berkeley, in U.S.A. Naturally, this involved many hardships, sacrifices, and deprivations for my family which cannot be repaid except by a deep sense of affection and devotion to them.

Finally, this inquiry is undertaken in utter humility and admiration, acknowledging the fidelity of the martyred Church of the Armenians in spite of long persecutions; and with modest pride for the Armenian contributions to world civilization—in the realm of politics, by its sons on the imperial throne of Byzantium; in military arts, by its generals in the Byzantine, Russian, and other armies; in fine arts, by its architecture which may well have been the prototype of the Gothic architecture of Europe: and in commerce, trade, agriculture, industry, crafts, and professions, by its many brilliant sons scattered in every corner of the earth.

Therefore, this book goes out not in the spirit of arrogant criticism but with a *deep desire to examine one* of the causes of Armenian historical tragedies; and with earnest prayer that it may become a humble contribution in the search for a solution of Christian and Muslim relations, in the name of Him who came to break down all walls of partition.

Perhaps one word would be permissible as to the value of such a study. It cannot be denied that the Monophysitic position of the Armenian, Syrian, and Egyptian Christians had a catastrophic consequence in the sweeping advance of Islam in the Middle East and the eventual downfall of the Byzantine Empire.

We do not need to quote many distinguished historians to confirm the fact that the monophysitic alienation and disintegration caused in the Middle East were large factors in the unhampered conquests by Islam.

As this paper deals only with one of these peoples (Armenians) who embraced the Monophysite Christology and thereby weakened the unity and strength of the Byzantine Empire and of the Universal Church to withstand the tide of Muslim advance, it is earnestly hoped that in the present era of atheistic communism and aggressive Islam the findings of this study might help to remind us of the *necessity* of achieving unity among the Christian peoples of the Middle East, *if* we want to stem the tide of these movements alien to the genius of the Christian gospel. It is further hoped that this research would be a small contribution to attack the *divisive* forces which have splintered the Middle Eastern Christians and thereby weakened and paralyzed them in their *fundamental mission*—to proclaim the Gospel of Christ to those who have not recognized His redeeming love, atoning death, and glorious resurrection.

Tonopah, Nevada   THE AUTHOR
1965

INTRODUCTION

The political and social revolutions in the Middle (or Near) East since World War II and the recurrent threats of resumption of fighting between the Arab League and Israel underline the perennial importance of this region for a lasting peace.

To recall some recent history, the nationalistic uprisings and declaration of independence of almost all of the former European colonies and mandated territories; the seizure and nationalization of the Suez Canal and the Iranian oil industry; the reception of Greece and Turkey into the NATO as a bulwark against communist advance into the Mediterranean basin; the civil war in Lebanon and the landing of U.S. Marines in Beirut; the assassination of the first king of Jordan; the repeated coup-d'état and murders in Iraq; the creation, dissolution, and recreation of a "United Arab Republic"; the most recent Cypriotic civil war and the threats of intervention by Turkey and Greece; and other unnamed conflicts and crises such as in Yemen and Aden—all are indications that the Middle East is a nerve center of world peace.

While Arab nationalism, economics, and social conditions play decided rôles in this area, the RELIGION OF ISLAM as a major factor cannot and should not be ignored. Granting that Arab consciousness has united the Christians and Muslims in the common cause of freedom and progress, it should be remembered also that, excepting Lebanon, the Christians of Near or Middle East constitute a very small minority in each country and that they have no other choice but to cooperate with the bloc of the dominant and ardent followers of ISLAM extending from Morocco to Pakistan and the Black Sea to the Sudan.

It is undeniable, therefore, that in the relations between the Arab nations and the West and the Arab League and the State of Israel, the Muslim faith and its outlook hold a central position. The dislike and hatred of the Christian West; the desire to rule rather than be ruled; the undeclared aspirations to revive the Muslim Empire of the Caliphs —all of these enter into the picture.

This situation is a reminder of the failure of the Christian churches of the Near East to evangelize their pagan and Muslim neighbors. When Muhammad emerged with his simple creed, sincere zeal for monotheism, and the sword, he captured the inhabitants of Arabia by his faith. His successors—within a century—swept over an entire continent of Christians with their innumerable churches. Eventually, Syria, Palestine, Persia, Mesopotamia, North Africa, Egypt, Sudan, Asia Minor, and Armenia were overrun and subdued by the Muslim-Arab rulers.

Among the Christians who survived the first shock of the Muslim invasions were those who possessed a strong national consciousness. The Armenians were one of these peoples who lived under the rule of Muslim Caliphs as *dhimmis*—that is, tributary subjects. The *dhimmis*

> were granted the protection of the state, which guaranteed them life, property, and security in the practice of their religion... In return they were obliged to pay a special tax known as the *jizyah* and to accept a subordinate position in the social... (and) political life of the community. They were set at a disadvantage by certain legal disabilities in regard to testimony, marriage, and protection under the criminal law... They were allowed to replace and rebuild churches, but not to erect new ones, and were commonly expected to conduct their rites in a manner inconspicuous and inoffensive to Moslems.[1]

Under these circumstances and restrictions the Christians were primarily concerned with their own safety and survival. Missionary endeavor among their conquerors *seemed* to be out of the question. Therefore, after thirteen hundred years of Christian contacts with Islam, today we still have to reckon with a solid Muslim bloc. In this failure all the Christian minorities of the Near East are equally blameworthy. The Armenians are one of these.

Many reasons have been adduced to explain this fact. Speaking of the Armenians, it has been said that (1) they were a *subject race* and captives of a hostile faith and state. Therefore, they were not in a position to exert any missionary effort among their Muslim rulers and neighbors.

However, many members of the early church of the Apostolic and post-Apostolic eras were social and political slaves.[2] And yet, through their witness and Christian conduct they exerted such a tremendous influence on the Roman Empire that within three centuries their faith was accepted as the state religion.[3] The early Christian witnesses in the

---

[1] J. T. Addison, *The Christian Approach to the Moslem: A Historical Study* (New York: Columbia University Press, 1942), pp. 20-21. Reprinted by permission of the publishers.

[2] Gal. 3:28; Col. 3:11; Eph. 6:5-9; P. Schaff, *History of the Christian Church* (New York: Charles Scribner's Sons, 1869), I, 112 f., 318 f.; K. S. Latourette, *A History of the Expansion of Christianity*, Vol. I, *The First Five Centuries* (New York: Harper & Brothers, Publishers, 1937), pp. 224 ff.

[3] Latourette, *op. cit.*, I, 128–57, 184, 191, 261 f.

traditions of the Armenian Church—St. Thaddaeus, St. Bartholomew, Princess Sandoukhd, St. Kayyane, St. Hripsime, and St. Gregory the Illuminator—were in no better circumstances, but their testimonies eventually won the Armenian rulers and the people to the Christian faith.[1]

2. It has been asserted that the *death penalty* imposed upon the Muslim converts to Christianity was the greatest deterrent of Christian missionary activity and success.[2]

Yet, the early apostles, evangelists, preachers, and the common believers continued their witness in spite of persecutions, tortures, execution, and even crucifixion. The fates of Apostles Paul and Peter during the Neronian persecutions;[3] or of the early Christian Church under Trajan, Decius, Marcus Aurelius, Diocletian, and other Roman Emperors, did not deter the preachers from spreading or the hearers from accepting the message of the Christian Gospel.[4] Furthermore, the Zoroastrian faith prescribed the same death penalty for apostasy, but many Persians accepted the Christian faith, and later embraced Islam despite the Zoroastrian opposition. Or again, the early Christians in Armenia did not face any less danger. Princess Sandoukhd was beheaded by her own father, King Sanatroug of Armenia (ca. 75–110 A.D.); St. Gregory was imprisoned by King Trdat (Tiridates) III (ca. 287–337 A.D.) for over ten years, but they persisted in their Christian affirmation.[5]

3. It might be said that an aggressive missionary attitude would have caused general persecution, endangering the national life and safety of the Armenians in Muslim lands.

Nevertheless, the early Christians risked everything for the gospel, their faith and fortitude winning sympathy and eventual victory for

---

[1] *Ibid.*, pp. 105 f., 223 f.; S. Der-Movsesian, *History of the Armenians* (Venice: St. Lazare Press, 1922), II, 12 ff.

[2] L. Arpee, *A History of Armenian Christianity* (New York: Armenian Missionary Association of America, 1946), pp. 78, 202 f.; Addison, *op. cit.*, p. 25; J. Richter, *A History of Protestant Missions in the Near East* (New York: Fleming H. Revell Company, 1910), pp. 171 ff.

[3] Latourette, *op. cit.*, p. 137 ff. J. C. Ayer, *A Source Book for Ancient Church History* (New York: Charles Scribner's Sons, 1924), pp. 6 ff., 9 f.

[4] H. B. Workman, *The Martyrs of the Early Church* (London: Charles H. Kelly, 1913), pp. 10–24; and his *Persecution in the Early Church* (London: The Epworth Press, 1923), pp. 197–282, 362–365; Ayer, *op. cit.*, pp. 22, 206, 258.

[5] L. E. Browne, *The Eclipse of Christianity in Asia* (Cambridge: The University Press, 1933), p. 63; Moses of Khorene, *History of the Armenians* (Venice: St. Lazare Press, 1881), pp. 240–245.

their message.[1] As for the threat to the national safety of the Armenians, over a million martyrs have been sacrificed for national and political aspirations; a few thousands could have been sacrificed for direct evangelization of the Muslims. This, in the long run, might have saved the million innocent men and women who were massacred in the nineteenth and twentieth centuries because of political aggressiveness.[2]

4. It could be argued, as Arpee has done, that the Muslim Turks, being a wild, cruel, and unprogressive tribe from Mongolia, were not open to the civilizing influence of Christianity.[3]

Again, it can be answered that the northern tribes of Goths, Visigoths, Vandals, Burgundians, Alamanni, Franks, Huns, Alani, Celts, Lombards, Bulgars, Avars, and Slavs, who invaded Europe in the Middle Ages, were no more tame or docile. In fact, the Bulgars and the Huns were of the same Mongolian extraction as the Seljuk Turks.[4] But the Church of Rome and the Eastern Orthodox Church had evangelized these wild tribes to become the Europe of today. Furthermore, in the eleventh century, Kerait tribe of Turks in northern Mongolia had accepted Christianity when a very large number of them had received baptism.[5] It is far more significant that modern England has descended from Celts and Anglo-Saxons, of whom the former "practiced magical arts and barbarous rites of human sacrifice,"[6] whereas, however wild and cruel, the Muslim Turks have not been accused of offering human sacrifices in their worship. Moreover, Arabs and Turks embraced Islam which was, and is, far superior to the Arabian and Mongolian pagan worship and cultures.[7] Lastly, the forefathers of the Armenians had their own wild traits and religious customs, such as offering slaves to

---

[1] W. Walker, *A History of the Christian Church* (Edinburgh; T. & T. Clark, 1930), pp. 86 ff., 108 ff.; Schaff, *op. cit.*, pp. 343 ff.; Ayer, *op. cit.*, pp. 7 ff., 258 ff., 281.

[2] Der-Movsesian, *op. cit.*, II, 738 ff. Cf. page 10, note 5 below.

[3] Arpee, *op. cit.*, p. 203.

[4] Latourette, *op. cit.*, I, 211–215; II. *The Thousand Years of Uncertainty, A.D. 500-A.D. 1500* (New York: Harper & Brothers, Publishers, 1938), pp. 5–6, 237 ff.; C. Eliot and A. N. J. Whymant, "Huns," *Encyclopedia Britannica*, ed. by J. L. Garvin, 14th edition, Vol. XI (1930).

[5] A. Mingana, *The Early Spread of Christianity in Central Asia and the Far East: A New Document* (Manchester: The University Press, 1925), *passim*; Browne, *op. cit.*, pp. 9, 102, 137 ff.

[6] H. M. Chadwick, "Britain (Anglo-Saxon)," *Encyclopedia Britannica*, ed. J. L. Garvin, 14th ed., Vol. IV (1930); Latourette, *op. cit.*, I, 209, 256; H. M. Gwatkin and J. P. Whitney (eds.), *The Cambridge Medieval History* (New York: The Macmillan Co., 1913), II, chap. XVI, pp. 496–542; "Celt or Kelt," *Encyclopedia Britannica*, Vol. V, 14th ed.

[7] Addison, *op. cit.*, pp. 260 ff.

the goddess Anahit,[1] but they were converted to the Christian faith, and, in turn, they evangelized the wild tribes of Iberians (Georgians) and Albanians of Caucasus.[2]

5. Finally, it has been stated that the moral laxity of the Islamic religion was more attractive to the Turks than the stern, puritanic, requirements of the Christian Gospel. Therefore, it is maintained, they were unwilling to yield their sensuous and formalistic practices for the higher, spiritual, faith and ethical conduct.[3]

There is much truth in this argument. The ethics of Islam is very poor. Nevertheless, the human heart reveals the same longings for spiritual satisfaction everywhere, even among the Muslims. The Sufis —the mystics of Islam—are witnesses to this fact.[4] The howling Dervishes seeking union with *Allah* (God) are eloquent examples of this inward need. A man like *Al-Ghazali*, for instance, the great mystic Muslim theologian of the eleventh century—died in 1111 A.D.—cannot be set aside by the argument that because of the moral laxity and sensuality of Islam he was not open to the message of the Christian Gospel.

6. Probably, the extremely deistic conception of God in Islam was one of the *major* obstacles to evangelism. Stressing the *otherness* of God, Muslims would find it hard to accept a Father-God whom the Christians worshipped. Furthermore, the spirituality of God as taught by the Christian faith was another stumbling block. To Islam, spirit is semi-physical, semi-material, and corporeal. Therefore, God as spirit is incomprehensible to the Muslim believer.[5]

However, neither of these causes is sufficient to account fully for the failure to win the Muslims to Christianity. The Hebrew conception of God was as monotheistic and the religion of Judaism as legalistic as

---

[1] Strabo, *Geography* (Loeb ed.; New York: G. P. Putnam's Sons, 1928), XI. xiv, 16.

[2] Arpee, *op. cit.*, p. 20; Khorene, *op. cit.*, pp. 168–170, 302, 358 ff.; Agathangelus, *History* (Venice: St. Lazare Press, 1930), pp. 382, 395, 408, 412, 420, 440.

[3] S. Zwemer, *Islam, A Challenge to Faith* (New York: Student Volunteer Movement, 1907), pp. 119 ff.; Arpee, *op. cit.*, p. 203.

[4] M. Smith, *Readings from the Mystics of Islam*. Translations from the Arabic and Persian, Together with a Short Account of the History and Doctrines of Sufism and Brief Biographical Notes on Each Sufi Writer (London: Luzac & Co., Ltd., 1950), pp. 59–73; L. Levonian, *Studies in the Relationship Between Islam and Christianity: Psychological and Historical* (London: G. Allen & Unwin, Ltd. 1940), pp. 42 ff.; D. B. Macdonald, *Aspects of Islam* (New York: The Macmillan Co., 1911), pp. 150 ff.; N. A. Faris, (ed.), *The Arab Heritage* (Princeton: Princeton University Press, 1944), pp. 142–158.

[5] Levonian, *op. cit.*, pp. 59–80; "Ruh," *A Dictionary of Islam*, 1 vol., 2nd edition.

in Islam. Jesus, as the messenger of the universal Fatherhood of God and His spiritual kingdom was rejected by the Jews.[1] Neither was the concept of spirituality very far advanced among the Jews. In fact, the psychological ideas of Judaism and Islam have a common source in their Semitic origins. Therefore, to the Jews also modern psychology and its interpretation of the spirit were alien.[2]

Again, the human soul and spirit were understood by the Hebrews in terms of the physical body and material substance. Nevertheless, Jesus' teaching on God as spirit and his spiritual interpretation of the law were accepted by the disciples and Saul of Tarsus, who were transformed into ardent followers and advocates of the new faith.[3]

Indeed, the Muslims of the seventh century or the seventeenth may have misunderstood the nature of the spirituality of God and of the human personality, but there were sufficient common beliefs between Christians and Muslims to bring them together—such as the majesty and unity of God, the supremacy of His will, the prophets, revelation, the holy books, Jesus the Messiah (*Isa al-Masih*), the resurrection, and the future judgment.[4]

The fact of the matter is that at the advent of Islam the Christians themselves, including the Armenians, had fallen to such low depths that they, too, had forgotten the spiritual nature of the deity. They had represented deity and Christ by physical and material objects—such as icons, relics, and external ceremonies—which would have made no appeal to the already non-spiritual, yet ultratranscendental, conceptions of the Muslim mind.[5]

This materialistic conception of the spirit led the Muslims to the misconception of sin and salvation. God being conceived as semi-corporeal and the human spirit as materialistic stuff, sin and salvation were interpreted physically and materially, or, at the most, intellectually rather than morally. To them, sin was legal and physical uncleanliness, and salvation physical purification. The Christian idea of sin as moral failure and salvation as moral uprightness did not enter Muslim theology. Even if sin were considered rebellion against God,

---

[1] John 4:24; Matt. 5:1 ff., chaps. 26–27.

[2] A. C. Knudson, *The Doctrine of Redemption* (New York: The Abingdon Press, 1933), pp. 94 ff.; Levonian, *op. cit.*, pp. 19–33.

[3] Acts 8:1 ff.; Phil. 3:5–8.

[4] *Infra*, chapter V, pp. 70 ff.

[5] W. F. Adeney, *The Greek and Eastern Churches* (New York: Charles Scribner's Sons, 1908), pp. 165 ff., 191 f.

this was without ethical content and personal responsibility. For, it was believed that God in His absolute might eternally decrees all—good or bad, pure or impure—and man is simply a tool, a toy, in the hands of the unchangeable, immutable, and absolute decrees of Almighty Allah.[1]

The only means to counteract this moral and spiritual error would have been an earnest spirituality on the part of the Christians. Unfortunately, the Christian churches and communions, including the Armenians, themselves had lost the sense of ethical sin and spiritual salvation. To them also sin had become externalized and salvation reduced to ceremonies, iconolatry, Mariolatry, and sacramentarianism. Naturally, such a religious attitude would have made no impact upon the Muslim mind and environment.[2]

The reasons set forth above appear to be insufficient to explain *fully* the failure of the Armenians and other Christians to evangelize their Muslim environment. We should search for a more fundamental hindrance than those enumerated, *valid as they are*. To this writer the Christology of the Armenian Apostolic Church seems to be a basic and fundamental obstruction on the part of the Armenian Christians. This thesis is an attempt to inquire into the relevance of the Armenian Christology to Armenian relations with their Muslim environment. *Granting the presence and rôle of other factors*, it maintains that the *Monophysite Christology of the Armenian Apostolic Church played a major role in the failure of Armenians to evangelize their Muslim neighbors*, in that:

> The *Monophysite Christology* constituted the basic cause of the *final break* of the Armenian Church with the Church of the Empire.
>
> *Monophysitism* and the consequent rupture transformed the Armenian Church into a *schismatic* institution, forcing it to self-defense, religious isolationism, dogmatism, ceremonialism, and sacramentarianism and sacerdotalism.
>
> *Defensive isolationism* led the Armenian Church to the *neglect of the opportunity* for aggressive evangelism in the non-Christian environment.
>
> Monophysitism *overlooked the appeal of the human life of Jesus Christ*, thereby obstructing the intellectual and practical avenues of approach to Islam.
>
> The *complete break* with the Church of the Empire, the *consequent persecutions*, and the need of self-defense *fully nationalized* the Armenian Church.

---

[1] Zwemer, *op. cit.*, pp. 95 ff.
A. S. Tritton, *Muslim Theology* (London: Luzac & Co., Ltd., 1947), pp. ff.; Levonian, *op. cit.*, pp. 71 f., 92, 93.
[2] Adeney, *op. cit.*, pp. 141 ff., 187 ff., 194–195.

Ultimately, the *religious isolationism* and *nationalism* led to *political isolation* and the tragedies of the Armenians in the nineteenth and twentieth centuries.[1]

The argument is developed in *five parts. Part one* deals with the ecclesiastical background of the Armenians. *Part two* traces the development of the Armenian Christology. *Part three* discusses the bearing of Christology on evangelism. *Part four* presents the relation of Christology to nationalism and politics. *Part five* ventures to suggest a possible re-orientation of the Armenian Church.

Two *types of sources* have been used: primary and secondary. The *primary sources* are the Armenian texts of the classical writers of the fourth, fifth, and sixth centuries, known as the Golden Age of Armenian literature:

1. Moses of Khorene, born in the second half of the fourth century, a clergyman and translator, was a native of the village of Khorny in the province of Taron (Daron); hence his name Moses *Khorenatzi*, i.e., of Khorny. He is also referred to as Moses Chorenensis. In this discussion he will be cited as *Khorene*. He wrote his *History of the Armenians*[2] in ca. 480 A.D., at the request of his superior, Catholicos Isaac. His sources are the legends, oral traditions, and the Armenian ballads of the province of Koghtn. He has been nick-named the "Armenian Herodotus." At times he is uncritical and inaccurate; yet, his work is the only extant source for the legendary origins of the Armenians. His narrative ends with ca. 437 A.D.[3] He has preserved many fragments from ancient Greek historians whose originals have been lost.

This work has been translated into French by Victor Langlois under the title of *Collection des Historiens anciens et modernes de l' Arménie*.[4] Also, F. N. Finck has repeated references to Khorene in his brief survey of the Armenian literature—"Geschichte der armenischen Litteratur"— in *Geschichte der christlichen Litteraturen des Orients* ("History of the Christian Literature of the Orient").[5]

2. *Agathangelus*, the historian of the fourth century, of Greek origin, was the secretary to King Tiridates III of Armenia. He has written his *History* to cover the period of ca. 226 (Khosroes II) to 330 A.D. (Tirida-

---

[1] For a pictorial illustration of the argument of this dissertation see *Infra*, Appendix, Diagrams A-K, pp. 136ff.

[2] Published in Venice: St. Lazare Press, 1881.

[3] Der-Movsesian, *op. cit.*, II, 169 f. Cf. page 10, footnote 5 below.

[4] Published in Paris: Z. Renan, 1867–1869, 2 vols.

[5] C. Brockelmann *et al*, *Geschichte der christlichen Litteraturen des Orients* (2nd ed. with corrections; Leipzig: C. F. Amelangs Verlag, 1909), pp. 75–130.

tes III).[1] He narrates the martyrdom of St. Gregory, St. Hripsime, and St. Kayyane; records *The Teaching of St. Gregory;* describes the conversion of Armenia and the voyage of St. Gregory and King Tiridates III to Rome (ca. 324).

This work is preserved in Greek and Armenian, the former relying on the latter. The comparison of the two texts has led scholars to conclude that there was an original version, now lost, on which both of the extant versions depend. The present text of Agathangelus is said to have been edited by a priest—Eznik—of the seventh century. It is included in Langlois' *Collection.*

3. Faustus of Byzantium lived and wrote in the fourth century. He, too, was of Greek origin. His *History of the Armenians*[2] covers ca. 344–394 A.D. He, with Moses of Khorene, has the most abundant material about the first two centuries of Christian Armenia. The original manuscript, now lost, was written in Greek. Faustus wrote a series on Byzantine history, of which the *History of the Armenians* was a section. This, likewise, is translated in the *Collection* of Langlois.[3]

4. Lazare of Pharbe was a soldier as well as a translator, born in ca. 440 in Pharbe, province of Ararat. He was descended from a noble family and was educated at the royal palace. He was one of the disciples of Isaac and Mesrop who were sent to Byzantium to study the Greek language. On his return he was appointed governor of the metropolis of Etchmiadzin. He wrote a *History of the Armenians and Epistle to Vahan Mamigonian,* dealing with the period up to ca. 485 A.D.[4] It is available in Langlois' *Collection.*[5]

5. Of the *doctrinal sources,* John of Otzun's (Otznetzi) *Tractate against the Phantasiastae* was written in ca. 719. It refutes the errors of the Docetists. John was the Catholicos of the Armenians at this time. His book is translated by Arpee in full.[6]

6. Gregory of Datev (Datevatzi) wrote his *Book of Questions* in ca. 1397, to refute the teachings of the Roman Catholic Uniates and the various heresies of the Christian Church.[7]

7. Lastly, Father A. Torossian, of New York, has translated the

---

[1] Published in Venice: St. Lazare Press, 1930. Cf. also Langlois, *op. cit.,* I, 99–193; Brockelmann, *op. cit.,* pp. 89 ff.

[2] Published in Venice: St. Lazare Press, 1933.

[3] Langlois, *op. cit.,* I, 302–310.

[4] Published in Venice: St. Lazare Press, 1933.

[5] Langlois, *op. cit.,* II, 253–368.

[6] Arpee, *op. cit.,* pp. 325–354.

[7] Published in Constantinople, 1729; Arpee, *op. cit.,* pp. 175–186.

Armenian Liturgy into English under the title of *The Divine Liturgy According to the Rites of the Holy Apostolic Church of Armenians*.[1] This is the third major-doctrinal-primary source to be cited in this discussion.

Of the *secondary sources* in Armenian, four will be listed here:

1. *National History*, by the late Archbishop M. Ormanian, former Patriarch of Constantinople, is a voluminous work covering the entire history of the Armenians from the beginning of the Christian era to the year 1909.[2]

2. *The Church of the Armenians*, by the same author, is a valuable summary of the history and teachings of the Armenian Church.[3]

3. *The Church of the Armenians*, by the late co-Catholicos Papken Guleserian of Antilyas, near Beirut, is a collection of essays dealing negatively with the problem of the reformation of the Armenian Church.[4]

4. *History of the Armenians*, by the Mekhitarist Father Sahag (Isaac) Der-Movsesian, a Roman Catholic, is a critical treatment of Armenian history.[5]

Of the *secondary sources in English*, only three will be mentioned here:

1. *A History of Armenian Christianity*, by Leon Arpee, is the most frequently quoted volume.[6] It is based on Der-Movsesian and Ormanian.

2. *Armenia: Travels and Studies*, by H. F. B. Lynch, is a masterly treatment of the people, land, customs, and Church, of Armenia.[7]

3. *The Key of Truth*, by F. C. Conybeare, is an invaluable study of the teachings of the Paulicians in Armenia. It contains the Armenian text and translation of the Rule of Faith of this heretical sect, with a long critical introduction by the author himself. He also has a Latin translation of the *Tractate* of John of Otzun.[8]

As for the use of names, although the official designation of the Armenian Church is The Holy Apostolic Church of Armenia, also called Gregorian, in this paper we shall use the abbreviated form—The Armenian Apostolic Church, or the Armenian Church.

---

[1] Published in New York: The Gotchnag Press, 1933.
[2] Published in Constantinople: V. & H. Der-Nersessian,1912–1914, Vol. I & II; Jerusalem: St. James Press, 1927, Vol. III.
[3] Published in Constantinople: V. & H. Der-Nersessian, 1913.
[4] Published in Jerusalem: St. James Press, 1930.
[5] Published in Venice: St. Lazare Press, 1922, 2 vols.
[6] New York, 1946; *supra*, p. 3, note 2.
[7] Published in London: Longmans, Green & Co., 1901, 2 vols.
[8] Published in Oxford: The University Press, 1898.

PART ONE

THE ECCLESIASTICAL BACKGROUND

CHAPTER ONE

A SKETCH OF THE ARMENIAN ECCLESIASTICAL RELATIONS

The ecclesiastical fortunes of the Armenians have not been any brighter than the political. At this point we should examine briefly the relations of the Armenian Apostolic Church with the Church of the Empire, as the historical antagonism between them is closely connected with the Christological position of the Armenian Church.

A. THE CONVERSION OF ARMENIA

The Armenians accepted Christianity as the state religion in ca. 301 A.D. Their pre-Christian religion was nature worship. Under the Persian rule, they had adopted the Mazdaist faith and its deities Ahura Mazda as Aramazt and Anaitas as Anahit, with such other native gods as Asdghig and Vahakn (Van Agni). Later, they adopted the Graeco-Roman deities, indentifying Aramazt with Zeus, Anahit with Artemis, Asdghig with Aphrodite, and Vahakn with Hercules. Therefore, when Christianity was introduced to Armenia the people lacked nothing in heathen worship, religious customs, and mores.[1]

The Armenian Church Fathers were convinced that the first preachers of the Christian Gospel in Armenia were St. Thaddaeus and St. Bartholomew.[2] Many legends, traditions, sacred spots, and historical allusions are cited as evidence. The legends of the correspondence of King Abgarus of Edessa with Christ[3] and the martyrdom of the virgins Kayyane and Hripsime, even though unhistorical, still testify to the belief in pre-Gregorian Christianity in Armenia.[4]

---

[1] M. H. Ananikian, "Armenia (Zoroastrian)," *Encyclopedia of Religion and Ethics,* Vol. I (1922).

[2] The Roman Catholics reject this claim. See V. Hatzooni's *Important Problems from the History of the Armenian Church* (Venice: St. Lazare Press, 1927), *passim.*

[3] Eusebius, *The Church History,* in *A Select Library of the Nicene and Post-Nicene Fathers of the Christian Church,* ed. P. Schaff and H. Wace (2nd series; New York: The Christian Literature Co., 1890), I, 100 ff., 291; F. C. Burkitt, *Early Eastern Christianity* (London: John Murray, 1904), pp. 11–20.

[4] Tertullian, *Latin Christianity: Its Founder, Tertullian,* in *The Ante-Nicene Fathers. Translations of the Fathers down to A. D. 325.* Ed. A. Roberts and J. Donaldson. (American Reprint of the Edinburgh Edition; revised; Buffalo: The Christian

However these may be, the actual national conversion occurred early in the fourth century. St. Gregory, the apostle of this missionary conquest, was reared and baptized in Caesarea of Cappadocia where he had been sent for refuge from the assassins of his father. Gregory's own father had murdered Khosroes II, the king, whose son Tiridates III, in whose reign the national conversion came to pass, as a child had found asylum in Rome from the murderers of his father.

When of age, Tiridates was granted the crown of his father and returned to Armenia with the assistance of Emperor Diocletian. On his way home, he engaged Gregory as an official of his palace. During a pagan festival Gregory refused to offer floral gifts to the goddess Anahit. Tiridates was sore vexed. Discovering that Gregory was the son of Anak, the assassin of his own father, he was further enraged and placed him in prison for over ten years. While in chains, Gregory was summoned to pray for the recovery of Tiridates from lycanthropy. His cure led him to accept the Christian faith and was baptized.

Now, Gregory and Tiridates joined hands to make Christianity the state religion of Armenia. Pagan temples were destroyed. Some of them were transformed into Christian sanctuaries. For lack of bishops to ordain him, Gregory was sent to Bishop Leontius of Caesarea and was consecrated as the Catholicos (Universal Bishop) of the Armenians. A solemn agreement was signed that future bishops of Armenia were to be ordained by the Bishop of Caesarea. This was the beginning of a permanent tie between the Eastern Orthodox Church and the Armenian Church.[1]

Gregory ruled as the first Catholicos of the Armenians until his death in 325 A.D. He established the hereditary episcopate in the Armenian Church. He was succeeded by his sons Aristakes (Rostaces, 325–333) and Vertanes (Bartanes, 333–341). Aristakes represented his father at the Nicene Council. Gregory died the same year, after receiving the Canons of Nicaea from the hands of his son.[2]

Vertanes was succeeded by his son Housik (341–347), but Housik's two sons—Bab (Pap) and Atanakine—refused the garb and office of

---

Literature Publishing Co., 1885), III, 157 ff.; Der-Movsesian, op. cit., I, 179–216; II, 13 ff.; Ormanian, National History, I, cols. 1–70; Khorene, op. cit., pp. 226 ff., 326 ff., 345 ff.; Arpee, op. cit., pp. 9 ff.

[1] B. J. Kidd, The Churches of Eastern Christendom From A.D. 451 to the Present Time (London: The Faith Press, Ltd., 1927), pp. 428 ff.; Lynch, op. cit., I, 276–314; Adeney, op. cit., pp. 539–542; Ormanian, National History, I, cols. 71–90; Der-Movsesian, op. cit., II, 5–18.

[2] Arpee, op. cit., pp. 9–23; Agathangelus, op. cit., passim; Ormanian, National History, I, cols. 71–118; Der-Movsesian, op. cit., II, 5–18.

clergy. Therefore, Paren (348–352), a disciple of St. Gregory, was elected to succeed Housik. However, his grandson, Nerses—the son of Atanakine—later renowned as "the Great," recovered the Catholicos-sate for Gregory's house. Nerses (353–373) was "Great" in his church-manship, Christian zeal, Christian benevolence, educational endeavors, and theological acumen.[1]

It was in the reign of Catholicos Isaac I (Sahag)—ca. 387–436—the son of Nerses the Great, that Mesrop of Mashdotz formulated the Armenian alphabet (ca. 403–406), and with a group of assistants he translated the Bible, the Greek Liturgy, and many authors of the West into the Armenian language, thus laying the foundations of a national literature.[2]

The immediate consequence of this literary movement was that the rank and file read the Scriptures in their own tongue; attended the divine services in their own language; and better grasped the deeper meaning of the teachings of Christ. So that, when Jezdegerd II wanted to reimpose his pagan faith on Armenia, Armenians refused to yield to Persian demands and took up arms to defend their religious liberty.[3]

For fifteen hundred years the Armenians have celebrated this war of freedom of conscience. The military defeat of 451 A.D. was transformed into moral victory by the treaty of toleration granted by Persia in 484. However, the Armenians were soon to face religious persecutions from another unsuspected corner—their co-religionists and neighbors of the Greek Church.

B. THE BREAK WITH THE GREEK CHURCH

The Fourth Ecumenical Council was held in Chalcedon in 451.AD. while the Armenians were engaged in their war of religious liberty with Persia. The Armenian Church was not represented at Chalcedon. Their Catholicos and nobility were in prison in the Persian capital when the Council of Chalcedon was summoned. Therefore, the de-cisions of the Fourth Council reached Armenia very late (ca. 490); they were misinterpreted as "Nestorian" and later rejected officially. Ever since that fateful day, the Armenian Church has been isolated and considered heretical with the other Monophysite churches of Egypt,

---

[1] Ormanian, *National History*, I, cols. 123–222.

[2] *Ibid.*, I, cols. 264–326; Arpee, *op. cit.*, pp. 24–42; Der-Movsesian, *op. cit.*, II, 153–174.

[3] Kidd, *op. cit.*, pp. 431 ff.;

Syria, and Ethiopia. Of course, this has not been conducive to cordial relations with the Eastern Orthodox (Greek) and the Western Catholic (Roman) Church. On the other hand, it has had strong bearing upon the political destiny of Armenia and the Armenians.[1]

We have seen that when St. Gregory was ordained by Bishop Leontius of Caesarea, a permanent relationship was established between the Armenian and the Greek churches. Unfortunately, King Bab (Pap) of Armenia (353–373) reversed this friendly relationship with Caesarea. He was suspected of poisoning Catholicos Nerses the Great, to set up a rival Catholicos—named Faustus (Housig or Shahag)—of the house of Bishop Albianus. This alienated Caesarea, forcing St. Basil (370–379) to refuse ordination and consecration of Faustus as Bishop of Armenia. Therefore, he was consecrated by Bishop Anthimus of Tyana, and thereafter no Armenian bishop was ordained in Caesarea. Thus Bab, a reckless and ambitious king, realized his purpose of the establishment of an independent, national, Armenian Church like the other national churches around Armenia.[2]

When Armenia was partitioned between Persia and Byzantium in the reign of Theodosius I (ca. 385), the seat of the Catholicossate fell under Persian rule. This provided the geographical and political cause for the final break of the Armenian Church with the Greek Church in Caesarea, as Bab's conduct had given the ecclesiastical and jurisdictional cause.[3]

Under these circumstances the Council of Chalcedon was convened while the Armenians were engaged in a war of survival. They had asked for military assistance of Theodosius II and Marcian, but were denied it. A treaty of friendship and neutrality between Theodosius and Persia had left the Armenians at the mercy of the latter. When the word of Chalcedon reached Armenia, their cool reception was quite understandable. For half a century Armenians had lived as though the Chalcedonian Council had not been held at all.[4]

However, in the year 506 A.D., in the reign of Catholicos Papken I (490–516), a delegation of orthodox Christians from Persia sought the

---

[1] Adeney, *op. cit.*, p. 552; Arpee, *op. cit.*, pp. 44–57; Lazare, *op. cit., passim*.

[2] Kidd, *op. cit.*, p. 430; Arpee, *op. cit.*, pp. 21 ff.; *Infra*, Appendix, Diagrams A, B, pp. 136 ff.; Ormanian, *National History*, I, col. 223; Faustus, *op. cit.*, pp. 230 ff.; Khorene, *op. cit.*, p. 228; *supra*, p. 14 f.

[3] Arpee, *op. cit.*, pp. 21 ff.; Khorene, *op. cit.*, p. 228; Faustus, *op. cit.*, p. 221; Der-Movsesian, *op. cit.*, II, 63–68, 192 ff.; Ormanian, *National History*, I, cols. 203–219; *Infra*, Appendix, Diagrams A, B, pp. 136 ff.

[4] Arpee, *op. cit.*, pp. 120–125; Ormanian, *National History*, I, cols. 338–345; Der-Movsesian, *op. cit.*, II, pp. 241 ff.; *infra*, chapter II.

advice of the Armenian hierarchy regarding the Nestorian Christians taking refuge in Persia. This gave the occasion for the ecclesiastical synod called at the capital city of Tevin, where the Catholicos, his twenty bishops, and fourteen nobles solemnly affirmed their adherence to the orthodox doctrine of Nicaea. They declared their creed to be that of the Ephesian Council, which, they claimed, asserted one unified nature of the Incarnate Word. Therefore, at this meeting in Tevin, they officially condemned the dual nature doctrine of the Chalcedonian formula, and anathematized Arius, Nestorius, as well as Eutyches.

In the year 551, in the reign of Catholicos Nerses II, a second synod was held at Tevin, which again condemned the Chalcedonian symbol and decreed to break every relation with the Greek Church, even to the point of adopting a new Armenian ecclesiastical calendar, 551 A.D. being its first year.[1]

Thus, the separation of the Armenian Church from the Church of the Empire, begun under Bab with the break with Caesarea and aggravated by the political situation, became a *permanent* and *incurable* breach because of doctrinal dispute.[2]

C. ATTEMPTS AT REUNION

Throughout its history many attempts have been made to reunite the Armenian Church with the Church of the Empire. The first step was taken by Emperor Heraclius in ca. 633 A.D. The Armenians had assisted him in capturing Jerusalem from the Persians. During his visit to the Holy Land, he invited Catholicos Ezras (Ezr) to negotiate the reunion of the two churches. Heraclius, being the supporter of the Monothelite formula, which confessed only one divine will operating in Christ, drew up a compromise statement without mentioning Chalcedon. A synod was called by Ezr in Garin (Erzeroum) which approved the agreement and a united Communion Service (Mass) was held (ca. 633).

On the basis of this accord the Armenians separated the feast of Christmas from Epiphany on January 6 and removed from the *Trisagion*—Thrice Holy—the Monophysite phrase "who wast crucified for us."[3] But the clergy and the people were provoked by the surrender

---

[1] Arpee, *op. cit.*, pp. 120–128; Ormanian, *National History*, I, cols. 366, 367; *Infra*, Appendix, Diagrams A–F, specially F, pp. 136 ff.

[2] *Infra*, chapter II; *Infra*, pp. 136 ff.

[3] This liturgical ascription, based on Isaiah's vision (ch. 6), originally read: "Holy God, Holy and Almighty, Holy and Immortal, have mercy upon us." To

of Ezr to Heraclius and the reunion was nullified.[1] Ezr had other worries also. The Arabs were at the gates of the capital city of Tevin which was soon captured and Ezr died during the siege. His immediate successor Nerses III (641–661) called a third synod at Tevin (ca. 645), where again Chalcedon was censured.

In 726, during the reign of Catholicos John of Otzun (717–728), Caliph Omar II called a meeting of Armenians and Syrian Jacobites in Manazkert where the two churches were merged into one on the basis of their common Monophysite doctrine.[2] Such an enforced merger was foreign to Armenian temperament and was soon broken.

The next attempt was made by Photius, the Patriarch of Constantinople, suggesting the acceptance of the Chalcedonian decrees. Scholars differ as to the outcome of this step. Some think a reunion was consummated at a council held in Shirakavan in 862.[3]

Others think this meeting denounced Chalcedon and thwarted the attempts of Photius.[4] Judging from the subsequent fact of continuous schism, the latter view seems to be nearer the truth.

D. Contacts in Cilicia

The Armenians came into direct contact with the Latin (Roman) Church during the period of the Crusades. Pope Eugenius (1145–1153) invited the Armenian Catholicos, Gregory III (1113–1166), and his church to submit to Rome, but the Pope received no satisfaction.[5]

In the days of Catholicos Nerses the Graceful (1166–1173), Manual Comnenus (1143–1180) invited the Armenians to reunite. A synod was called at Hromkla (in Syria), where Assyrians, Greeks, Latins, and Armenians gathered to consider reunion. Emperor Manual could not attend in person but he sent two clergy representatives with nine chapters of conditions:

> (1) To anathematize those who say "one nature" of Christ,... (2) To confess two natures, two wills, and two operations in Christ. (3) To re-

---

this, the Monophysites had added the phrase "who wast crucified for us" just before the words "have mercy upon us." See further *infra*, chapter III, section C, p. 49 f.

[1] Arpee, *op. cit.*, pp. 131 ff.; Kidd, *op. cit.*, p. 432; S. Der Nersessian, *Armenia and the Byzantine Empire* (Cambridge: Harvard University Press, 1945), pp. 39–40; Ormanian, *National History*, I, cols. 686–706.

[2] Adeney, *op. cit.*, pp. 545 ff.; Ormanian, *National History*, I, cols. 837 ff.

[3] F. Macler, "Armenia (Christian)," *Encyclopedia of Religion and Ethics*, Vol. I (1922).

[4] Der-Nersessian, *op. cit.*, pp. 40–42; Ormanian, *National History*, I, col. 670.

[5] *Ibid.*, I, cols. 1366–1399; Arpee, *op. cit.*, pp. 131 ff.; Ormanian, *The Church of the Armenians*, pp. 88–89.

move from the *Trisagion* the conjunction "and" and the words "wast crucified." (4) To celebrate the Christian feasts with the Greeks: the Annunciation on March 25; Christmas on December 25; the Circumcision on January 1; the Baptism on January 6; the Presentation on February 2; and to change the Dominical feasts and those of the holy virgin Mother of God, John the Baptist, the holy Apostles, and other saints. (5) To prepare the *Muron* (chrism) with olive oil. (6) To use leavened bread and mixed wine at the Communion. (7) During the Mass and other services of worship to keep the congregation in the church, excepting those who are on penance. (8) To accept the canons of the fourth, fifth, sixth, and seventh general councils... (9) To submit the election of the Armenian Catholicos to the approval of the Emperor.[1]

Nerses agreed, in principle, to this offer of reunion. A long negotiation was conducted but he died before it was consummated. His successor, Krikor IV (Gregory, ca. 1175), rejected the nine chapters as unacceptable. Comnenus reduced them into two—namely, the acceptance of Chalcedon and the dual nature doctrine. Krikor called a second meeting in Hromkla and drew up a compromise statement himself, but before it reached the hands of the emperor, death intervened. The successor of Comnenus—Emperor Isaac II Angelus—reversed the policy of friendly negotiation. On the contrary, he forced the Armenians of the Empire to consent to reunion to the point of inflicting severe persecutions on them. He coerced three bishops and sixteen hundred priests to accept Chalcedon.[2]

Under Prince Leo II, the possibilities of a reunion were further explored. As he was anxious to be crowned king of Cilicia, he consented to the following demands laid by Pope Innocent III (1198–1216), who had him crowned as the King of Armenia on January 6, 1199:

(1) To celebrate the Dominical feasts and the feasts of the saints according to the fixed calendar and cancel the Armenian calendar. (2) To perform the divine service in the sanctuary (as the Armenians celebrated the Mass in the Church, while the rest of the liturgy was performed in the courtyard because of Arab brigandage). (3) To use only fish and oil, but no milk or meat, during the Christmas and Easter fasts; (4) to teach the Armenian children the Latin language; and (5) to send to the Roman Pontiff a delegate of the Catholicos at regular intervals as a sign of submission and to bring the gifts of the Armenians to Rome.[3]

---

[1] Ormanian, *National History*, I, col. 1432. *Used by permission.*

[2] *Ibid.*, I, cols. 1410–1451; Der-Nersessian, *op. cit.*, pp. 42–50; Arpee, *op. cit.*, pp. 141–148; Ormanian, *The Church of the Armenians*, pp. 90–91.

[3] Ormanian, *National History*, I, col. 1535*; Arpee, *op. cit.*, p. 149, gives the date of Leo's coronation one year earlier, namely, 1198 A.D.

* *Used by permission.*

However, no sooner had the ink dried than Leo expelled the Latin clergymen from Cilicia.

Leo's successor, Hetum II, a strongly Latinophile king, set up a Latinophile Catholicos—Krikor (Gregory) VII. Krikor planned to revise the Armenian Church, its liturgy, as well as Armenian doctrine on the Roman pattern, but death interrupted his scheme. His successor pursued the same policy of friendship with the Latins. This was quite displeasing to the surrounding Tartars, Turks, and Egyptians. Therefore, the Egyptians attacked Cilicia and terminated the Armenian kingdom of Cilicia (1375).[1]

However, the activities of the Roman Catholic Church did not cease. Franciscans continued to preach Catholicism in Cilicia. A "Society of Uniates" was organized. A delegation of this group attended the Florentine Council of 1439. The Council named the uniates "The United Church of Armenia." Their missions extended to the interior and Constantinople, where, eventually, an Armenian Catholic Patriarchate was set up in 1835 in the reign of Sultan Mahmoud II.[2]

After the fall of Constantinople in 1453, Sultan Muhammad II devised the "millet" system whereby the civil and religious affairs of the Christian minorities of the Ottoman Empire were entrusted to the care of their respective ecclesiastical heads: The Chalcedonians under the jurisdiction of the Greek (Eastern) Orthodox Patriarch, and the anti-Chalcedonians under the authority of the Armenian Patriarchate, which was created by Muhammad II in 1461. This system prevailed until it was abolished by the Turkish Republican government after World War I.[3]

E. RUSSIAN INFLUENCE

When Caucasus was occupied by Russia in 1828, the Catholicossate of the Armenian Church residing in Etchmiadzin remained within the Russian territory. Consequently, the Russians intervened and secured the supremacy of the Catholicos of Etchmiadzin over the Armenian Patriarch of Constantinople. Secondly, the Czarist régime imposed upon the Armenian Church certain governing principles for its administration, decreed in 1836 and known as *Polojenye*. Among other

---

[1] Ormanian, *The Church of the Armenians*, pp. 92–98.

[2] *Arpee, op. cit.*, pp. 157 ff., 256–265; Adeney, *op. cit.*, pp. 547 ff.; Der-Movsesian, *op. cit.*, II, 721 ff.

[3] E. G. Mears, *Modern Turkey* (New York: The Macmillan Co., 1924), pp. 98, 121–123, 419–420, 518; Adeney, *op. cit.*, pp. 548 ff.; Kidd, *op. cit.*, pp. 434 ff.

rules, it imposed that the Armenians should nominate and submit the names of two archbishops, one of whom the Czar would appoint as the Catholicos and the other as his vicar. This law was in force until the rise of the communist régime in Armenia (1920). At present, the Armenian Church in Soviet Armenia is subject to the same restrictions as all others in Soviet Russia.[1]

F. THE PRESENT STATUS

At this writing, the Armenians in Syria, Lebanon, and Cyprus are under the jurisdiction of the Catholicos of Cilicia which was created during the Rubenian Kingdom of Cilicia in the eleventh century. This see was transferred to Antilyas, near Beirut, Lebanon, after World War I. Those in the Holy Land are under the spiritual care of the Patriarch of Jerusalem, which was established in 1311. The remnants in Turkey, mostly in Constantinople, are shepherded by the Patriarch of Constantinople. The rest in Europe, the Americas, Egypt, and Asia, are under direct jurisdiction of the Catholicos in Etchmiadzin. However, the above-mentioned three sees recognize him as their superior.[2]

G. THE ARMENIAN EVANGELICAL MOVEMENT

To come out of its isolation, the Armenian Apostolic Church needs to take some radical steps, which neither the clergy nor the laity are willing to face.[3] However, one aspect of Armenian life, namely, the Armenian Evangelical Movement, has partly solved that problem for itself.

The first Armenian Protestant church, called The Evangelical Church of Armenia, was organized in Constantinople on July 1, 1846. This was the continuation of the historical process of awakening among the Armenians in cultural, literary, political, and religious spheres of life.[4]

---

[1] Arpee, op. cit., pp. 298–299; Kidd, op. cit., p. 434; Ormanian, National History, II, cols. 1827–1830; Der-Movsesian, op. cit., II, 650 ff.

[2] Ormanian, The Church of the Armenians, pp. 164–165.

[3] See infra, chapter VII.

[4] J. Richter, A History of Protestant Missions in the Near East (New York: Fleming H. Revell Co., 1910), pp. 43–45; Arpee, op. cit., pp. 266–292; Y. S. Kassouny, The Path of Light: History of the Armenian Evangelical Movement (Beirut: Armenian Missionary Association of America, 1947), pp. 11–31; Ormanian, National History, III, cols. 3720–3725; Der-Movsesian, op. cit., II, 727; L. Arpee, The Armenian Awakening: A History of the Armenian Church, 1820–1860 (Chicago: The University Press, 1909), passim.

The events that we have traced briefly had reduced the Armenian Church to a dogmatic, ceremonialistic, conservative, and nationalistic institution. Its spiritual light was dimmed. Political, national, and factional feuds had sapped the moral and spiritual vitality of the Armenian Apostolic Church.[1]

But the Spirit of God was moving. A group of people, yearning for spiritual experience and church reform, had organized themselves into a secret "Society of the Pious", or an "Evangelical Union." The reigning Patriarch of Constantinople, Stephen, had blessed and supported them.[2]

At this juncture the first missionaries of the American Board of Commissioners for Foreign Missions arrived in Constantinople. They opened schools for the Armenian children. They encouraged the "Society of the Pious." They attended the divine services and preached in the Armenian Church. Their policy was to revitalize the Christian churches of the Near East and evangelize the Muslims through them.[3]

Unfortunately, the ruling class of the laity was alarmed by this awakening. They set out to suppress it. The Patriarch had to resign and a successor—a fanatic—was appointed. His one aim was to extirpate the new movement. Anathema, excommunication, imprisonment, flagellation, boycott, exile, expulsion from homes, refusal of marriage and burial, defrocking and banishment, were used to intimidate the "Pious."[4]

The outcome was the official organization of the Evangelical Church of Armenia. The British Ambassador acting as the intermediary, Sultan Abdul Medjid granted a royal *firman* (edict), recognizing this new group as the "Protestant *Millet* (religious community)."[5]

Following the official recognition, the movement advanced rapidly. Protestant churches were organized in every city and town of any im-

---

[1] R. Anderson, *History of the Missions of the American Board of Commissioners for Foreign Missions to the Oriental Churches* (Boston: Congregational Publishing Society, 1872), I, 90–140; II, 1–58; E. Smith, *Researches of the Rev. E. Smith and Rev. H. G. O. Dwight in Armenia* (Boston: Crocker & Brewster, 1833), II, 290–292.

[2] Anderson, *op. cit.*, I, 90 ff.; Arpee, *A History*, pp. 266 ff.; Arpee, *Armenian Awakening*, pp. 96, 99 ff.

[3] Anderson, *op. cit.*, I, 90 ff.; Richter *op. cit.*, pp. 66–88, 72; Arpee, *A History*, pp. 266 ff.; Adeney, *op. cit.*, p. 550; Prime, *contra'*, *passim*, specially pp. 126 ff., 171 ff.; Ormanian, *National History*, III, cols. 3720 ff.; Ormanian, *The Church of the Armenians*, pp. 120 ff.; Kassouny, *op. cit.*, p. 49.

[4] Anderson, *op. cit.*, I, 105–119, 386–416; Arpee, *A History*, pp. 267 ff.; Kassouny, *op. cit.* pp. 32–57.

[5] Anderson, *op. cit.*, I, 412 ff.; II, 1–9; *used by permission*. Kassouny, *op. cit.*, pp. 37 ff.

portance. The missionaries identified themselves with the work of the Protestant Church, although continuing to serve the entire country and the Armenian community with their schools, colleges, seminaries, hospitals, and dispensaries.[1]

The massacres of 1894–1896 and 1909 greatly reduced the number of Protestant Armenians in Turkey. Eighty per cent of them were massacred during the deportations of 1915–1916. The remnants expelled or self-exiled from Turkey are taking new roots in Syria and Lebanon, France, the United States, and in many other countries.[2]

Because of their early association with the Congregational missionaries, most of the Protestant Armenians have been affiliated with the Congregational-Christian fellowship.[3] Through the contacts with the American Board they have kept their world missionary interest. The Armenian Protestant churches in the Near East have a strong Evangelical Union which was represented at the Amsterdam Assembly of the World Council. The Armenian Protestants in the United States have an Armenian Missionary Association which cooperates with the American Board in a limited manner, that is, only in the work for and among the Armenians.

Although the Armenian Protestant Church has partially broken the chain of the self-isolation of Armenian Christians, still it has not been able to remedy the basic weakness of the Armenian Apostolic Church.

---

[1] *Ibid.*, pp. 58–105; Addison, *op. cit.*, chap. 8; Arpee, *A History*, pp. 269–278; Prime, E.D.G., *Forty years in the Turkish Empire*, (New York, 1877) pp. 315 ff., 330 ff., 425 ff.

[2] Arpee, *A History of Armenian Christianity*, p. 277.

[3] Now "United Church of Christ".

PART TWO

THE
CHRISTOLOGY OF THE ARMENIAN
APOSTOLIC CHURCH

CHAPTER TWO

THE DEVELOPMENT OF THE CHRISTOLOGY OF THE ARMENIAN APOSTOLIC CHURCH

Our survey of the ecclesiastical relations of the Armenian Church has pointed to the fact that the final break of this historic church with the Greek as well as the Roman Church on Christological grounds resulted in its religious and ecclesiastical, as well as political, isolation. Now we are ready to trace in detail the development of the Armenian Christology and its consequences.

A. ADOPTIONISM

The centrality of Christ for the Christian faith and the Church was recognized at the very opening of the New Testament era. St. Peter's confession, "Thou art... the Son of the Living God"; St. Paul's "keno-tic" statement, "who being in the form of God... humbled himself"; and St. John's *Logos* idea, "...the *Logos* was God... and the *Logos* was made flesh," are just a few of the New Testament emphases on the highly exalted and unique place of the person of Jesus Christ. Christology was the theological attempt—or a department of theology—interpreting this belief and formulating the doctrine of the person and work of Christ.[1]

Generally speaking, the Christological disputes centered around two approaches. The first was the Judaistic-Ebionitic emphasis which stressed the humanity of Christ and the necessity of adhering to the Mosaic law on the part of Christ's followers. The divinity of Christ was considered to be God's special gift to him.

The second was the Gnostic-Docetic approach which denied the Incarnation and the reality of the humanity of Christ. All subsequent controversies revolved around these two poles: whether Christ was only a human being elevated by God to divine honors, or He was solely a Divine Being and the Incarnation simply an appearance.[2]

The orthodox doctrine of the person of Christ was the *via media*,

---

[1] Matt. 16:16; Phil. 2:6–8; John 1:1, 14; Wilhelm Pauck, "Christology," *An Encyclopedia of Religion*, ed. V. Ferm, 1 vol. (1945).

[2] G. P. Fisher, *History of Christian Doctrine* ("International Theological Library"; New York: Charles Scribner's Sons, 1901), pp. 48, 51, 52–60.

affirming that both divinity and humanity dwelt in him perfectly.

The first of these interpretations was also known as Adoptionism, implying that Christ was born as an ordinary human being, but divine powers were granted him at his baptism as a reward for his perfect obedience to God. This teaching would destroy the *universality* of Christ, making him a Jewish prophet *selected* as Messiah, and Christianity a Jewish sect. The Gnostic-Docetic view would destroy the *distinction* of Christ and Christianity from other heathen religions wherein philosophy and mythology interpreted the universe dualistically; matter was considered evil; pure and absolute Being could not dwell in brute matter which was evil; therefore Incarnation was not possible and real; and Christianity was nothing distinct from philosophical speculation and knowledge.[1]

Thus, Adoptionism, Judaistic in its origins, advocated the theory that Christ was *made* the Son of God at his baptism as a reward for his obedient life. Some writers have pointed to traces of this teaching in the New Testament.[2]

The earliest advocates of this doctrine were Theodotus the Tanner, of Byzantium (ca. 190), and Artemon of Rome (ca. 230–270), who preached in Rome. However, the most ardent exponent of it was Paul of Samosata, Bishop of Antioch (ca. 260–272)—a protégé of Queen Zenobia of Palmyra. Paul was condemned by his orthodox opponents at a synod in Antioch in 269 A.D. His followers were accused of heresy by the Council of Nicaea under the name of "Pauliani."[3]

Paul's school of thought was also known as Dynamic Monarchianism, emphasizing the unity rather than the Trinity of God, thus leaving no room for a preexistent Son.[4] The Modalistic Monarchians, on the other hand, considered the Trinity as modes or manifestations of the one God rather than personal distinctions in the being of God. Sabellius, who taught in Rome in ca. 215, was the most distinguished exponent of this view. Therefore, it is also called Sabellianism.[5]

This adoptionistic teaching seems to have been held by the Armenian Christians before Nicaea. F. C. Conybeare and L. Arpee hold this view.[6]

---

[1] *Ibid.*, pp. 51, 98 ff.; A. C. Knudson, *The Doctrine of Redemption* (New York: The Abingdon Press, 1933), pp. 294 ff.

[2] *Ibid.*, pp. 287 ff.; cf. Acts 2:30–36; Luke 24:19; 7:16, 39; 13:33; Mark 6:4.

[3] Walker, *op. cit.*, p. 72 f.; Arpee, *A History*, p. 10.

[4] Knudson, *op. cit.*, p. 288.

[5] Walker, *op. cit.*, pp. 72 ff.; F. C. Ensley, "Monarchianism." *An Encyclopedia of Religion*, ed. V. Ferm, 1 vol., 1945.

[6] Conybeare, *op. cit.*, *passim*; Arpee, *A History*, pp. 9–14.

The following paraphrase of a quotation from St. Gregory suggests this idea:

> The Spirit... coming down at the Baptism... gave to Jesus the glory which became His.... John the Baptist, as the depository of Divine favors, conferred these favours of priesthood, prophecy, and kingship, upon our Lord Jesus Christ.[1]

Lynch quotes Bishop Archelaus of Edessa (275–277), one of the main sources of the teachings of the Armenian Church:

> Tell me, over whom it was that the Holy Spirit descended like a dove? Who is this one whom John baptizes? If He was already perfect, if He was already the Son, if He was already Virtue, the Holy Spirit could not have entered into Him; a kingdom cannot enter into a kingdom. Whose was the voice which came from heaven and bore testimony to Him: 'This is my beloved Son, in whom I am well pleased?'[2]

This quotation is specific in stating that the perfection and the Sonship of Christ resulted from his baptism, "giving voice to a strong current of orthodox opinion in his Church, as opposed to the docetic teaching of Mani..."[3]

The Armenian Church shows its adoptionistic background in its celebration of the feasts of Christmas and Epiphany jointly on January 6. This practice indicates the conception that the physical birth of Jesus was not as important as his spiritual birth and adoption at baptism. Therefore, St. Sahag I, the Catholicos of Armenians (387–436), did not include in his canons the feast of Nativity.[4]

Adoptionism was named by the Armenians "Messalianism" and "Borboritae"—*mdzghnoutiun, porporidon*—meaning "obscenity" and "sodomy." The Messalians were a mystic body holding semi-Pelagian views, exalting the freedom of man and living rather promiscuously. They were severely persecuted for their immoral conduct.[5]

Our earliest primary sources of Khorene and Agathangelus are silent about the history of the pre-Gregorian era, excepting the casual references to legends. This may be due to Adoptionism which was

---

[1] Conybeare, *op. cit.*, Introduction, pp. cxi–cxii; *Agathangelus, op. cit.*, pp. 315 ff.

[2] Latourette, *op. cit.*, I, 105; Lynch, *op. cit.*, I, 281*; Conybeare, *op. cit.*, Introduction, pp. xcii, xcvi–ci.

[3] Lynch, *op. cit.*, I, 281; *used by permission.*

[4] "Epiphany, Feast of," *Encyclopedia Britannica*, Vol. VIII, 14th ed.; Lynch, *op. cit.*, I, 284; Arpee, *A History*, pp. 9 ff., 105 ff.

[5] Conybeare, *op. cit.*, Introduction, pp. civ, cix; Ormanian, *National History*, I, cols. 296–297, 331–332.

* *Used by permission.*

condemned by the Nicene Council. Apparently, post-Nicene Armenian writers have not wanted to disgrace their nation by recording its heretical past. Thereby, unwittingly they have deprived us of an essential phase of Armenian history.[1]

B. Armenian Orthodoxy, ca. 325

St. Gregory might well have been an Adoptionsit, even though ordained at Caesarea. However, when the Nicene Council convened, his son Aristakes represented him and his Church. When Aristakes returned with the Canons of Nicaea, they were officially adopted by the Armenian Church before the death of Gregory in 325 A.D.[2]

There are no records to prove whether the Armenian Church was represented at the Second General Council held in Constantinople (381). Whether it was or not, the canons of this council were adopted.[3]

Thus, by adhering to the Canons of Nicaea and Constantinople, the Armenian Church accepted the Trinitarian formula of the "consubstantiality of the Son with the Father," and the divinity of the Spirit, "who together with the Father and the Son is adored and glorified."[4]

Likewise, we have no evidence that the Armenians attended the Third General Council in Ephesus (431 A.D.). However, they accepted it as ecumenical and its canons were approved. In fact, the hierarchy of the Armenian Church maintains that *only* the first three General Councils were truly ecumenical and binding, insisting that after Ephesus the Church was no more at one. Therefore, they claim that the decisions of Chalcedon and the succeeding councils were not valid and binding. On this ground the Armenian Church has claimed *orthodoxy*, and with its tradition of apostolicity, it has asserted that the Armenians have remained faithful to the unity of the Church of Christ while the others have abandoned it at Chalcedon.[5]

C. After the Council of Ephesus, ca. 431

As indicated above, the reign of Catholicos Sahag I (387–436) was a period of Armenian literary labors and transformation. In 426 he had

---

[1] Arpee, *A History*, pp. 10–15.

[2] Conybeare, *op. cit.*, Introduction, pp. cxi–cxii; Ormanian, *National History*, I, cols. 92–94, 112–115.

[3] Ormanian, *The Church of the Armenians*, pp. 51 ff.; Guleserian, *op. cit.*, p. 161.

[4] Father C. Raab, *The Twenty Ecumenical Councils of the Catholic Church* (London: Longmans, Green & Co., 1937), pp. 6, 10, 12, 30–31; *used by permission*.

[5] Ormanian, *National History*, I, cols. 494–5 ff.

Arpee, *A History*, pp. 28–43.

sent six young students to study Greek in Byzantium. At the conclusion of the Council of Ephesus, Maximian, the Patriarch of Constantinople, forwarded to Sahag the Canons of Ephesus, together with a Greek New Testament and an Old Testament in the Septuagint Version (432 A.D.). These were dispatched by the six students returning home, and were for the translation of the Scriptures into Armenian.

Immediately, Sahag called a special synod at Ashtishat (423), where the decrees of the Third Council were officially adopted. At a second synod in the same city (435), the bishops of the Armenian Church formally condemned Nestorius and the writings of Theodore of Mopsuestia—a distinguished predecessor of "Nestorian" views.[1] Practically speaking, Nestorius divided Christ into a duality in which the divine and the human were eternally distinguished; God the Word and human Jesus existing "always... (in) an intimate conjuction."

The bitterest enemy of Nestorius was Cyril, Patriarch of Alexandria (ca. 412–444). Following the Alexandrian school, he emphasized the unity of the nature of Christ, the human having been made fully divine. Although he held that the humanity of Christ was complete with body, soul, and spirit, and thus officially opposed Apollinarian views, yet he was quite close to them. Apollinaris had held that the Incarnation was the indwelling of the *Logos* in Jesus as a perfect man, as God dwelt in a temple, and that "in Jesus the place of the soul was taken by the Logos."[2]

> He, accordingly, who was born of the Virgin Mary was Son of God by nature and truly God... only according to the flesh from Mary was He man, but at the same time, according to the spirit, Son of God; and God has in His own flesh suffered our sorrows.[3]

This meant honoring the divinity but denying the humanity of Christ.

To Cyril, the real personality of Christ was the *Logos*. The *Logos* had taken flesh and clothed Himself with humanity. The divine in Christ was the result of the union of the two natures. While interchanging their qualities, each was complete, and from the two natures was formed the personality of Christ; that one personality was the divine. Cyril's position is clear in his famous twelve anathemas.[4]

This meant that "it was God made flesh... born... died..."[5]

---

[1] Ormanian, *National History*, I, cols. 310–313; Khorene, *op. cit.*, pp. 258–260; Ormanian, *The Church of the Armenians*, pp. 135, 166; Arpee, *A History*, p. 31.

[2] Walker, *op. cit.*, p. 144 f., 146.

[3] Ayer, *op. cit.*, p. 144 ff., 146, 496. *Used by permission.*

[4] Walker, *op. cit.*, pp. 143, 146.

[5] *Ibid.*

Thus, the Alexandrian school advocated an impersonal humanity while the Antiochian separated the divine and the human, making Christ Son only by adoption.

To Nestorius, the Incarnation was the indwelling of the Divine Logos (Word) in the man Jesus. To him, God could not be born, did not suffer or die.[1] He was striving to preserve the distinction of the human and the divine in Christ, maintaining that only flesh can be born of flesh. "For, that which is born of flesh is flesh."[2] On the other hand, to Cyril it was God made flesh, who was born, and died.

We cannot enter into the details of the Council of Ephesus where Nestorius was condemned for teaching the doctrine of the two natures residing in Christ with an unmixed union. Emperor Theodosius called the meeting which convened on June 22, 431 A.D.; Cyril presided; Nestorius was deposed; Patriarch John of Antioch, friend of Nestorius, condemned Cyril; the Papal legates confirmed the deposition of Nestorius; he retired to a monastery; and Theodosius, after some hesitation, confirmed the conviction of Nestorius, forcing the two contending parties—Alexandrian and Antiochian—to agree on a compromise statement of faith drawn up by Antioch.[3]

Cyril signed this creed; Nestorius was banished; a truce was reached, but the controversy did not die. Now the Nestorians were outlaws and under persecution. They took refuge in Syria and Persia and penetrated into China and India.[4]

The Council of Ephesus was led by the Cyrillian view of *"one nature of the Incarnate Word"* which was divine. *This phrase is central in the Christology of the Armenian Church*, as we shall soon notice.[5]

As already noted, the Armenian Church heartily assented to the decisions of Ephesus. By adhering to the Canons of Ephesus, they declared their orthodoxy as members of the "one, catholic, apostolic, holy Church," holding its common confessions and recognizing its three General Councils.[6] The Armenian opposition to the Nestorians was firmly expressed by Sahag I in his correspondence (ca. 434–435) with Proclius, the Patriarch of Constantinople, stating that these here-

---

[1] Raab, *op. cit.*, p. 16; H. R. Percival, "The Seven Ecumenical Councils" (in) *The Nicene and Post-Nicene Fathers*, XIV, 192–198, 207–215.

[2] Ayer, *op. cit.*, p. 501. *Used by permission.*

[3] Raab, *op. cit.*, p. 19 f.; Walker, *op. cit.*, p. 147.

[4] Walker, *op. cit.*, p. 149.

[5] Raab, *op. cit.*, p. 20.

[6] Ormanian, *National History*, I, cols. 22–38, 311; Guleserian, *op. cit.*, pp. 161–168, specially p. 163; Arpee, *A History*, pp. 12, 31, 102.

tics were condemned and that orders were given to expel from their country the "obstinate schismatics"; that they were not found in Armenia, but "if it should appear, doubtless we shall endeavor to uproot the swine."[1] The same assurances were given to Patriarch Acacius at a later date (ca. 471–489).

By its adherence to the decrees of Ephesus, the Armenian Church was decidedly opposing Nestorianism, which divided the person of Christ into a duality of the divine and the human natures. However, while thus it was uniting and agreeing again with the Church of the Empire, Ephesus was also to mark the end of an era and the beginning of a new one for the Armenian Church. For, soon it was to go on its own way in Christology, protesting its loyalty to the three General Councils and arguing that Chalcedon broke up the unity of the Church.[2]

D. CHALCEDON AND AFTER, CA. 451

The Council of Chalcedon was convened in the reign of Joseph I, the Catholicos of Armenians (ca. 437–452). It met on October 6, 451 A.D., at the call of Emperor Marcian and Empress Pulcheria. The major issue at this gathering was the teachings of Eutyches, an ardent Cyrillian.[3]

Eutyches, an old Archimandrite of Constantinople, in his zeal against Nestorian dualism, had gone to the other extreme of identifying and unifying the person of Christ, to the extent of making his flesh divine. He openly preached Cyril's doctrine of "one nature of the Incarnate Word." Hence the name *Monophysite*—one nature.[4]

The other chief actors at Chalcedon were Dioscorus, Patriarch of Alexandria; Pope Leo I; and Flavian, Patriarch of Constantinople.[5]

By the order of Emperor Theodosius II a preliminary meeting was held at Ephesus (449) where Eutyches was declared orthodox and Flavian deposed.[6] Only the supporters of Eutyches were in attendance there. On the death of Theodosius, Marcian and Pulcheria called the Chalcedonian Council, which repudiated the gathering of Ephesus, accepted the dual nature formula, re-instated Flavian, and convicted

---

[1] Ormanian, *National History*, I, cols. 311–313. *Used by permission.*
[2] Ormanian, *The Church of the Armenians*, p. 135.
[3] Ormanian, *National History*, I, col. 494.
[4] Raab, *op. cit.*, p. 24.
[5] Percival, *op. cit.*, pp. 243–296.
[6] Raab, *op. cit.*, p. 27; Walker, *op. cit.*, p. 150 f.

Eutyches of heresy. Pope Leo's letter to Flavian, known as "Leo's Tome," had defined the orthodox position on Christology as follows:

> We teach that one and the same Christ, the Lord, the only begotten Son consists of two natures, without confusion, without change, without separation, without division.[1]

The Council officially adopted this formula and on that basis convicted Eutyches of heresy.

Again, we are not sure whether the Armenians were invited to Chalcedon or not. This being the year and period of their war of religion with Persia, it is doubtful that any delegates could have attended it even if they were officially invited. Therefore, for a long while they were not in a position to be concerned with doctrinal disputes in the Empire.[2] However, two decades after peace was restored between Armenia and Persia (484–485 A.D.), the Armenian Church took action, rejecting the Chalcedonian formula and settlement.

There were other dissenters who had protested at Chalcedon and refused submission. The delegates of the Coptic Church in Egypt, the Syrian Jacobites, and the Abyssinians refused to accept the decree of Chalcedon, insisting on "the one incarnated nature of the Divine *Logos*." To them the Cyrillian Christology was paramount, which meant that God became man, abstractly in two natures, but really in one.[3]

On the basis of this Cyrillian definition some have called the Armenian Church "Cyrillian" rather than "*Monophysite*."[4] The Armenians rejected the Chalcedonian symbol for fear of Nestorian implications of dualism. They were firmly set on the doctrine of the *unity of the nature of Christ* as established at Ephesus.

Furthermore, they had accepted Zeno's *Henoticon* (ca. 482) which was a compromise instrument to unite Rome and Byzantium. The latter, under Emperor Basiliscus, had favored the *Monophysite* position, creating friction between Rome and Constantinople.[5] To reconcile them, the *Henoticon* had declared that Jesus Christ is

> Himself God incarnate, consubstantial with the Father according to His Godhead and consubstantial with us according to His manhood... He is... one Son, not two;... His miracles and the sufferings... endured

---

[1] Raab, *op. cit.*, p. 30 f.*; Walker, *op. cit.*, p. 151; Ayer, *op. cit.*, pp. 511–521.

[2] Der-Nersessian, *op. cit.*, pp. 32 ff.; Khorene, *op. cit.*, pp. 566–567; Ormanian, *National History*, I, cols. 340 ff.; Lazare, *op. cit.*, pp. 114 ff.

[3] Walker, *op. cit.*, pp. 153 ff.; Fisher, *op. cit.*, pp. 152 ff.

[4] Arpee, *A History*, p. 369.

[5] Adeney, *op. cit.*, pp. 111–112.

* *Used by permission.*

in the flesh are one... everyone who has held or holds any other opinion, either at the present or at another time, whether at Chalcedon or in any synod whatever, we anathematize.[1]

On the basis of this definition, B. Kidd believes that the Byzantine Church had become officially *Monophysite*. For, this meant the setting of Cyril's Twelve Articles of Anathemas against the dualists decidedly above the Tome of Leo I.[2]

When the Armenian Synod of Tevin in 506 A.D. denounced the Chalcedonian decrees, Georgian and Albanian bishops joined in it. In his second epistle to the Christians in Persia, Catholicos Papken I (490–516), affirming the Nicene creed, censured Nestorius and advised them "to flee from the apostates of the Nestorian lies of Chalcedon and others like them."[3] Likewise, with others he anathematized Eutyches, indicating that the Armenians were *Monophysites* in the Cyrillian rather than the Eutychean sense. Thus, by their rejection of the Chalcedonian symbol, the Armenians sided once for all with the Cyrillian formula—"*one nature of the Incarnate Word.*"[4]

Papken's decision was epochal for the Armenian Church. By it, the synod of 506 was breaking all relations with the Church of the Empire.[5]

The Armenian Fathers suspected Nestorian, Jewish, and pagan errors in the Chalcedonian settlement. They were also well aware of the jurisdictional rivalry of different bishoprics hidden under the Christological disputes. Therefore, they refused to be a party to Chalcedon.[6]

The action of the year 506 was also significant for the autonomy of the Armenian Church. It was made the archstone of the independence, perpetuation, and complete nationalization of the Armenian Church. It was also a major factor in the relations of the Armenians with their Muslim environment.

The effect of the break with the Church of the Empire was twofold: On the one hand, it isolated and weakened the Armenian Church. On the other hand, it was the means of keeping the Armenian Church as a national heritage. This dual consequence of the Christological break

---

[1] Ayer, *op. cit.*, pp. 528–259. *Used by permission.*

[2] Kidd, *op. cit.*, p. 17; Fisher, *op. cit.*, p. 156.

[3] Ormanian, *National History*, I, cols. 502 ff.

[4] Ormanian, *The Church of the Armenians*, p. 57; Der-Nersessian, *op. cit.*, pp. 37 ff.; italics supplied. In Armenian this phrase reads: "*Mi pnoutioun Panin Marmnatzelo.*"

[5] Bishop Tiran, *The Doctrinal Position of the Armenian Church* (New York: Armenian Diocesan Office, 1947), p. 8; Ormanian, *National History*, I, col. 514; Arpee, *A History*, pp. 120–125; *infra*, pp. 136 ff., Diagram F.; *supra*, pp. 15 ff.

[6] Ormanian, *National History*, I, col. 514.

of the Armenians is frankly acknowledged by the late Patriarch of Constantinople, Archbishop M. Ormanian, who admits that the break was the cause of "its (church's) isolation and separated weakness." "But," he continues,

> more than that consequence it is certain and will remain certain that it served as the means by which it remained as a national possession and the cause of its permanence and imperishable protection.[1]

As the break of the Armenian Church with the Church of the Empire was based on the Christology of the Chalcedonian Council and the Armenian refusal to submit to it, *Archbishop Ormanian admits the contention of this thesis that the Christology of the Armenian Church was a major cause of the isolation and weakness as well as the nationalization and permanence of this historic and martyred Church.*[2]

A recent writer, Miss S. Der-Nersessian, approaching the problem from another angle, makes the same admission as to the role of Christology in the Armenian Church and the rôle of the Church for Armenian nationalism. After surveying "the political relations of Armenia with the Byzantine Empire," she refers to the religious persecutions of the Armenians by the Greek Church and the Empire, maintaining that they were intended "to eliminate the autonomous Armenian Church, the main stronghold of Armenian nationalism."[3] Further on, speaking of the Christological controversies and the failure to come to an understanding, she continues:

> But the Armenians feared that by uniting with the Greeks they might lose their independence. The Byzantine Emperor and the clergy wished to abolish the autonomy of the Armenian Church; the clause included in the demands presented by Theorianus whereby the Catholicos was to be appointed by the emperor, is a patent proof of this. Nor could the Armenians forget the persecutions suffered at the hands of the Greeks.
>
> In a country partitioned among its powerful neighbors, internally divided by the rivalry of the princes... the church was the principal factor of national unity and the Greeks were well aware of this. The church not only maintained the community of faith but it also preserved the national language and literature, and thus became the stronghold of Armenian nationalism.[4]

---

[1] *Ibid.; Used by permission.* Tiran, *op. cit.,* p. 8 (see note 5, p. 35).

[2] *Supra,* p. 15 f.

[3] *Armenia and the Byzantine Empire,* p. 28, *Used by permission;* See note 4 below for full acknowledgement.

[4] Der-Nersessian, *op. cit.,* p. 52; Reprinted by permission of the publishers from Sirarpie Der-Nersessian, *Armenia and the Byzantine Empire,* Cambridge, Mass.: Harvard University Press, Copyright, 1945, by The President and Fellows of Harvard College; Latourette, *op. cit.,* I, 356.

Thus it seems that the Christology of the Armenian Church has served as one of the major causes and factors in creating and preserving the Armenian Apostolic Church as a national institution.[1] Politically and ecclesiastically, the Armenian Kingdom and its church had already drifted farther and farther from the Byzantine Empire.[2] The spirit of independence, autonomy, and nationalism launched by the intrepid soldier King Bab (Pap) was now institutionalized by the Church. The aim of an Armenian independent church was realized. The *Monophysitic* schism raised a citadel around it. The Greek persecutions forced the Church into the arms of the nation. Now the Church and nation were identified. Doctrine, institution, and nationalism became bulwarks against proselytization of every sort—Eastern Orthodox, Roman Catholic, or Muslim.[3] Ecclesiastical autonomy, Monophysitic distinction, and national survival so dominated the mind of the Armenian hierarchy that at times the leaders did not hesitate to ally themselves with the Muslim Arabs—as in the reign of Mahmed Jafar—against Byzantine coercions.[4]

To stress further the doctrinal divergence, separation, and national character of the Armenian Church, Nerses II, at a second synod in Tevin (551), on the one hand again anathematized the Nestorians who had smuggled into Armenia as merchants from Persia, publicly condemning their disorderly conduct;[5] on the other, he "established the Armenian calendar and once for all stayed out of communion with the Greeks."[6] On this centennial of the Council of Chalcedon the calendarial break with the Church of the Empire further deepened and widened the chasm already existent.[7] Henceforth the Armenian Church was so earnestly Monophysite and nationalized that all attempts at a reunion were of no avail.

The political implications of Chalcedon are obvious. It destroyed, once for all, the leadership of Alexandria in the East, long the rival of Constantinople. By Canon 28 Constantinople was raised to equality with Rome which Pope Leo I protested. The bishopric of Jerusalem was elevated to the standing of patriarchate which it had claimed with Constantinople, Alexandria, and Antioch.[8]

---

[1] Latourette, *op. cit.*, I, 106.

[2] Conybeare, *op. cit.*, Introduction, p. cxii.

[3] Der-Movsesian, *op. cit.*, II, 65; Adeney, *op. cit.*, p. 544; Arpee, *A History*, pp. 21 ff.

[4] Der-Movsesian, *op. cit.*, II, 691.

[5] Ormanian, *National History*, I, col. 546.

[6] *Ibid.*, I, col. 553; *supra*, p. 15 ff.

[7] Arpee, *A History*, p. 128.

[8] Raab, *op. cit.*, p. 32; Walker, *op. cit.*, p. 153.

Armenians were among the dissenters from Chalcedon. As followers of the Alexandrian school, the victory of Leo I over Dioscorus and Alexandria was displeasing to the Armenians. They were unwilling to recognize a Council where Rome, aspirant to supremacy over all churches, was dominant.

Further, to them Chalcedon represented the Antiochian-Nestorian view of Christ. The rivalry with Antioch would not permit the Armenians to accept the Antiochian position, thereby jeopardizing their own prestige.

Finally, the Byzantine Empire and its Church had sat back and watched the single-handed struggle of Armenia against Persian Mazdaism. Now *they*, the Armenians, were unwilling to recognize a Council called and supported by their Christian neighbors who were so indifferent to their plight.

All of these, however, were brought to a head by the Christological and soteriological fears that the Chalcedonian formula would turn the divinely wrought redemption to simply a human achievement. Therefore, Chalcedon was rejected unequivocally.

The Armenian Church, with its Catholicossate under Persian rule, could not consent to a doctrinal settlement which was interpreted as Nestorian and which was officially welcomed and encouraged by the same power—Persia—that had aimed at destroying the Armenian Church.

Again, the Armenians, with half of their people and their Catholicos living under Persian domination and the other half under Byzantium, could not very well endorse Chalcedon and thus seem to be uniting with the Byzantine and Roman world, further inviting the suspicions of the Persian Shah.

Last of all, with their inborn ambition for religious as well as national and political independence, the Armenians could not very well accept the doctrinal and moral supremacy of Rome and Byzantium when their own Armenian Church seemed to them to have equal claims to apostolicity, orthodoxy, and catholicity.

Therefore, the Armenian Church decided to denounce the Chalcedonian settlement. It was a serious decision. For, repudiating Chalcedon, the Armenian Church chose the path of religious isolationism, persecution, and self-defense. Naturally, the persecutions by the Empire and its Church, and the consequent coercions aroused the spirit of fervent nationalism, identifying the Church with the nation. Thereafter, the Armenian Church chose as its supreme task the preservation of its ecclesiastical independence through its Monophysitic differentiation, and the conservation of national identity by preserving the national language, literature, education, and traditions. The doctrinal isolation of the Church of Armenia and the consequent persecutions by the Greek Church forced the Armenian Church and its people to national pride, solidarity, and resistance. Forthwith, the rising nationalism of the Armenians, and other Monophysites, was used as a shield to protect their Monophysitic doctrine and thereby their independent, national church. After the loss of the political kingdom of Armenia, the Catholicos of the Armenian Church discharged the dual functions of the religio-political head of the nation. Thenceforward, his major task was to preserve intact the Armenian Church, and through the Church to conserve the Armenian culture and national identity.

Unfortunately, however, the net result and outcome were the contrary. Even though the Armenian Church preserved itself and the identity of the nation, in the long run it nearly lost the population which it was called to shepherd.

This intimate relation of Christology to nationalism and vice versa has been emphasized by one of the younger bishops of the Armenian Church—Bishop Tiran of New York,[1] whose pamphlet has been already quoted. He maintains that the nationalism of the Near Eastern, and Armenian, churches served as shield for Monophysitism. In other words, nationalism was used to defend the doctrinal position of the Armenian Church, not Monophysitism to defend nationalism.[2]

The obverse point of view is expressed by the late Archbishop Guleserian, who asserts that doctrine was used to prevent the assimilation of the Armenian Church, and through the Church to preserve national identity.[3]

Summarizing the development and consequences of the rupture of the Armenian Church with the Church of the Empire, we note:

(1) The Armenian Church, by its doctrinal dissent, was forced to self-isolation and self-defense. In the face of the consequent Greek and Roman coercions to conformity, it used every ounce of energy and strength to withstand the encroachments of the Church of the majority and to preserve its own identity.

(2) The *independence and autonomy* of a national Armenian Church conceived and initiated by King Bab (ca. 371) severed the Armenian

---

[1] *Formerly* of New York, transferred since 1952.
[2] Tiran, *op. cit.*, p. 8.
[3] Guleserian, *op. cit.*, p. 286.

relations with the Bishop of Caesarea, but it was unable to break the bonds of fellowship of the Armenian Church with the Church of the Empire. For, the independent Bishopric of Armenia officially joined the Church of the majority in approving and accepting the canons of the Second General Council held in Constantinople (ca. 381).[1]

(3) Nor again was the final breach effected by the *complete nationalization* of the Armenian Church through the creation of a national alphabet and literature (ca. 403). For, the canons of the Third General Council, forwarded to Catholicos Sahag I by Patriarch Maximian (432) were cordially received, approved, and adopted. Furthermore, St. Sahag I joined hands with Patriarch Proclius to extirpate the heresy of Nestorianism from Armenia.[2]

(4) When, however, the Fourth Council (451) defined the person of Christ by the dual-nature formula, the Armenians rejected and condemned it as a "Nestorian" teaching. What *ecclesiastical autonomy and nationalization* had not been able to do was accomplished by doctrinal suspicion, divergence, and dispute. Other subtle motives were present, as they were in all the controversies of Arianism and Nestorianism throughout the Church of the Empire, yet they were not powerful enough to sever and isolate the Armenian Church. But when doctrinal suspicions were aroused, the decisive step was taken, and the Armenian Church completely broke its ties with the Church of the Empire, even if it were to lead to the path of almost lonely religious isolation.[3]

(5) Once the doctrinal break was complete, the Armenian Church was persecuted and coerced by the Church of the majority. Therefore, the already independent, autocephalous, and nationalized Church of Armenia chose no other alternative but to identify itself with the nation and its interests, *using them* as shields to preserve its Monophysitic doctrine and ecclesiastical identity, and thereby guarding the Armenian national identity.[4]

(6) Now the church was on the way to becoming the bulwark of Armenian nationalism. The Empire and its Church threatened persecution and assimilation of the Armenian autonomous church. Therefore, to save its own existence from assimilation with the Greek Church, it clung tenaciously to its Monophysitic doctrine, using it as an impregnable wall of separation between itself and other churches.

---

[1] See *infra*, Appendix, Diagrams A, B, C, pp. 136 ff.
[2] *Ibid*, D.
[3] *Ibid*, E-F.
[4] *Ibid*, G-I.

(7) Keeping itself doctrinally distinct and unassimilated, the Armenian Church served as the saving ark of the Armenian national heritage—its language, literature, traditions, and racial identity. And the more it was persecuted the more it cherished its ecclesiastical individuality and its national identity. Thus, Monophysitism preserved the Church and the Church preserved the Armenian national consciousness and integrity.

(8) Thenceforth, whenever the Church was attacked and coerced to doctrinal conformity, the nation was at its side to fight for its ecclesiastical freedom and independence. And when the nation was attacked and endangered, the Church was at its side, to inspire its people to fight for the preservation of its national culture, consciousness, faith, and heritage.

It appears, therefore, that the Monophysitic Christology has preserved the Armenian ecclesiastical autonomy; the Church has conserved the Armenian national culture and heritage; and the Armenian nation has cherished, loyally supported, and defended, its Church at the cost of blood.[1]

---

[1] *Ibid*, H-I.

CHAPTER THREE

THE MONOPHYSITISM OF THE ARMENIAN CHURCH

Having dealt with the historical development and consequences of the Monophysitism of the Armenian Church, we should examine at a closer range the contents of the Christology of this ancient church.

Ormanian, Arpee, Miss Der-Nersessian, and others have insisted that the Armenian Monophysitism is Cyrillian, not Eutychean. We should, therefore, first take a look at the Cyrillian Christology again.

A. The Cyrillian Monophysitism

As stated before, Cyril's famous formula was "one nature of the Incarnate Word." His Twelve Anathemas against Nestorius make it explicit that the Incarnate Word was God in flesh.[1]

Cyril's position emphasized the divinity of Christ. While repudiating Apollinaris, he ascribed to Christ an Apollinarian "impersonal humanity." For his followers in Egypt Christ's humanity was absorbed in his divinity.[2]

Apparently Eutyches was convinced that his views were those of Cyril and the holy Fathers.

We cannot say what position Cyril would have taken had he been living and present at Chalcedon, where the following creed was adopted:

> Following the holy Fathers, we all with one voice teach men to confess that the Son and our Lord Jesus Christ is one and the same, that He is perfect in godhead and perfect in manhood, truly God and truly man, of a reasonable soul and body, consubstantial with His Father as touching His godhead, consubstantial with us as to His manhood, all things like unto us, without sin... in two natures, unconfusedly, immutably, indivisibly, inseparably; the distinction of natures being preserved and concurring in one person and hypostasis, not separated... or divided, into two persons, but one and the same Son and only begotten, God the Word, the Lord Jesus Christ.
>
> . . . .[3]

---

[1] Ayer, *op. cit.*, pp. 505–507; Percival, *op. cit.*, pp. 201 ff.; 206 ff.

[2] Ayer, *op. cit.*, pp. 513–514.

[3] Ayer, *op. cit.*, p. 520. *Used by permission.*

This definitely rejected the Cyrillian interpretation of the hypostatic union. Obviously, Cyril was uniting the natures of the *Logos* and Jesus, to make him one divine-human person, while Chalcedon was keeping the two natures distinct, co-existent, and operative in the divine-human Christ. Cyril was endeavoring to preserve the divine aspect of the Incarnate *Logos*; Chalcedon was aiming at preserving the human characteristics with the divinity. Cyril was thinking in terms of the Greek, mystical, conception of salvation, mortality transformed into immortality by the union with the divine. Chalcedon was following the Latin emphasis of right relations and forgiveness rather than mystical union with the divine.[1]

Ormanian and others, while trying to exonerate the Monophysitism of the Armenian Church as Cyrillian rather than Eutychean, are forgetful of the fact that Cyril's Christology itself is erroneous, and that in his teaching the Incarnate Word is not truly human with a human rational spirit. To Cyril, Christ has a human body and soul, but his ego, the mind, is the *Logos*, the Word of God, who controls his flesh.[2]

We should now turn to the evidences of this Cyrillian Monophysitism in the teachings of the Armenian Church. We shall confine ourselves to the internal evidences, as the external proofs are abundantly given in the writings of the ancient as well as modern historians.[3]

B. Monophysitism of the Doctrinal Writings

1. *St. Gregory the Illuminator, ca. 325*

We cannot gather much material from Gregory's writings, as he belongs to the Nicene age. As mentioned before, he might have been an adoptionist.

However, in *The Teaching of St. Gregory*, recorded by Agathangelus in his *History*, we have the germs of the Monophysite doctrine. Speaking of the Incarnation, he says:

> Though it was for us he descended to lowliness, yet he remains and continues in his own nature even as he himself says, 'I am the same, and have not changed.'[4] For though he took upon himself the image and

---

[1] *Ibid*, pp. 505–507; Walker, *op. cit.*, p. 41.

[2] Ayer, *op. cit.*, pp. 505–507.

[3] To mention a few moderns, Frederic Macler, the French Academician, in *Encyclopedia of Religion and Ethics*, I, 803 ff.; Adeney, *op. cit.*, chap. VI; Kidd, *op. cit.*, Chap. XVII; Latourette, *op. cit., passim*. All writers accept the fact that the Armenian Church is Alexandrian in its Christology.

[4] Agathangelus, *op. cit.*, pp. 191 ff.; 277–280; Arpee, *A History*, p. 60.

flesh of man, yet did he mix, unite and merge that flesh with his deity...
Though he assumed flesh, and descended to our likeness, yet he con-
tinues forever in that nature of his deity which he derives from the
Father....[1]

These quotations need no further comment. Without realizing it, St.
Gregory was laying the foundations of the Monophysitic Christology
of his church.

2. *Catholicos John of Otzun (Otznetzi, ca. 717–728)*

John of Otzun has been considered the staunchest defender of
Monophysitism. We are indebted to Arpee for the English translation
of John's *Tractate against the Phantasiastae* (Docetists), which is a defence
of the Armenian Church and its doctrine against these heretics.[2]

John's interpretation of the Incarnation of the *Logos* and his Christology are identical with those of Gregory of Datev, whom we shall take
up next. To John the Docetic falsehood is the worst. Nothing "could
be worse than denying Christ to have come in the flesh."[3] This they do
for fear that

> they should convey the idea of two natures in the one Christ. (But)...
> if Christ could indeed bear the passions of the flesh without the flesh,
> why then did he at all assume flesh of the Virgin, by a nine months'
> gestation, and appear, being born, as an infant?[4]

The Docetists answer that "he did not become flesh *of* the Virgin, but
in the Virgin, ... it was God the Word made flesh in the Virgin's
womb."[5] John asserts that the Incarnate Word was born *of* the Virgin,
of a woman, *of* Mary, and *not in* the Virgin.[6]

The fear of two natures leads the Docetists to the error of confessing
that the Word was changed into flesh and bones. To John, the nature
of the flesh and the nature of the Word are not one because of identity
of natures, "nor God the Word derived His being from Mary," but
"coming down from the uncreated Father, assumed an acquired flesh
of the Virgin's womb." Therefore, to him, one nature of the Incarnate
Word meant that the Word became "man and being known as such,
remained God, and man in becoming God... lost not his own substance."[7]

---

[1] Agathangelus, *op. cit.*, pp. 190 ff., 277–280; Arpee, *A History*, p. 60.
[2] Ormanian, *National History*, I, col. 835; Arpee, *A History*, pp. 325–354.
[3] Arpee, *A History*, p. 326.
[4] *Ibid. Used by permission.*
[5] *Ibid.*, p. 326 f. *All quotations used by permission.*
[6] *Ibid.*, p. 327.
[7] *Ibid.*, pp. 327, 328.

This meant that each nature "is constant in that which it possessed in the beginning."[1] However, the point is, what happens to the dual natures *after* the Incarnation? John affirms that a unity of everything takes place in Christ, who is one person, one self, one nature. In Christ,

> ...the incorporeal Word... assumed flesh of Mary, that is our human nature, and uniting it with his own person and nature, became... one person and one nature, including his flesh... The Word from the Father, united it (the human nature) with his own perfection... to be one perfect being, possessed of one soul and one personality... the perfections of the two natures in view of their union, and... the perfection of the unity... a unity in immutability, and an immutability in unity.[2]

John is explicit that the Word and the human flesh do not co-exist but are immutably united into one in Christ.

Briefly, then, John's doctrine of the unity of the nature and the person of Christ meant not the identity of natures or uniformity of personality but the "ineffable union of the Word with his own body." The Word "was united with the fleshly nature, and assumed the flesh into his divinity."[3]

On the strength of these statements Miss Der-Nersessian has concluded that John accepted the dual nature in Christ.[4] But she has not followed him to the end where he asserts the unity, the ineffable union, of the natures in the Incarnate Word. For, according to John,

> The Word was not changed into the nature of the flesh nor was the flesh changed into the nature of the Word, but each, while continuing and being known in the properties of its own nature, manifests... the *nature of the Son to be one.*[5]

By the same token, the maintenance of the two natures would mean confessing Christ "as both God and Man." "How, then, canst thou say that he became man and died, or caused by his death the gift of immortality to flow to usward?"[6] Even to the holy Fathers, according to John, "the mystery of the Incarnation... and the unity of the Incarnation" meant that

> He hungered... thirsted... wearied... slept... according to the flesh; neither thereby did he compromise his Deity, but rather manifested the nature of his flesh... Yet in the nature of his Deity he can neither suffer nor want, but is the Fulfiller and the Perfecter of all creatures.[7]

---

[1] *Ibid.*, p. 328.
[2] *Ibid.*, p. 329.
[3] *Ibid.*, p. 329.
[4] Der-Nersessian, *op. cit.*, p. 39.
[5] Arpee, A History, p. 328.
[6] *Ibid.*, p. 334.
[7] *Ibid.*, pp. 335, 336.

Using nature as substance as well as nature, Catholicos John believed that the one nature of Christ was the divine, and "the impassible One suffered in that part of Him which was passible."[1]

3. *Gregory of Datev (Datevatzi, died, ca. 1410)*

Gregory of Datev lived in the period of Tamerlane. He was a theologian in the monastery of Datev in the province of Siunik. His *Book of Questions* was completed in 1397, during the second Tartar invasion of Armenia. It was published in Constantinople in 1729–1730. He has used the Scholastic method to fight the Uniates of Armenia. This work has been named the Armenian *Summa*.[2]

After refuting the heretics of his time—the Arians, Macedonians, and Docetists[3]—he attacks the Nestorians,

> who deny the unity of the nature of God incarnate, but say that only by co-habitation and by the grace of adoption the Incarnate rose to the glory of Deity.[4]

Gregory asks them:

> If God Incarnate became man, then why do you deny and divide into two natures the God and the Man?[5]

If Christ had two natures, then, Gregory asks,

> which nature in Christ is to be worshipped? If the divine, you worship as a Jew... If the human nature only (is to be worshipped), you fall under blasphemous man-worship; and instead of worshipping the creator, you worship the creature, contrary to divine laws .   .   .   .   .   .
>
> Which nature of Christ is One Lord? If the divine only, then you fall into (the error of) Arius.... But if the human only you say (is the One Lord), then you deprive the Word of Lordship.
>
> . . . .
>
> By which nature do you call Christ the Son of God? If you say by the divine nature, then you would say his humanity is by grace. But if you say that He is the Son by the human nature, behold you deprive the Word of Sonship. But if both, behold you say that two natures exist in the Father.[6]

Next, Gregory takes up the *perfection* of Christ and asks whether it resided in his *person* or *nature*:

---

[1] *Ibid.*, pp. 347, 324, 334.

[2] *Ibid.*, pp. 175, 176–186; Ormanian, *National History*, II, col. 1982.

[3] Gregory of Datev, *Book of Questions* (Constantinople, 1729–1730), pp. 7–60. *Used by permission.*

[4] *Ibid.*, p. 66b; 67a. *All quotations used by permission.*

[5] *Ibid.*, p. 68b.

[6] *Ibid.*, pp. 68b–69a.

...Do you say perfect of the person or of the nature? If (you say) of the nature, then you admit two perfections into the Trinity, because the Trinity is one perfect nature, to which you add one nature of man. But (if you say) perfect of the person, behold you make the Trinity a Quaternity, so to say.[1]

As for the actual *Incarnation*, Gregory inquires:

...Did the Virgin Mary bear the only begotten Son by himself and the first born separately, and both? For, if both, behold you said (she is) mother of two sons. But if only the first born, behold the Son born of the Virgin you do not call God, following Nestorius. And if (she bore) only the Word, then you conclude the beginning of his existence as from the mother and not from Father God.[2]

He further asks whether the divine Son sat at the right hand of God, came down from heaven, and was born of the Virgin, or the human son by grace.[3]

Then Gregory emphatically asserts the *unity* of the nature of Christ, using many proof texts from the Scriptures, and concludes:

...One is our Lord Jesus Christ and God born in flesh of the Virgin. That when we say the Word became flesh it means the unity of the Word and flesh... *God the Word became flesh, but remained the Word.* And the Word became flesh by uniting with the flesh; therefore, it is evident that the flesh of the Word became the Word by the same union. Then, *therefore, the body of Christ is God.*[4]

To Gregory, therefore, "Christ is true God united in the body, eternally indivisible."[5] To admit two natures in him would amount to worship either the divine nature of Christ as God, or the human nature and fall into anthropolatry; to deny the essential divinity of the Son and fall into Arianism; and to add a fourth person to the perfect nature of Trinity.

As for the relation of the one nature to the Trinity, just as man has the common human nature as well as individuality,

so God the Word has the same nature of divinity in His individuality, and only He is united with the flesh, but not the Father and Spirit...[6]

In regards to the indivisible essence or substance of the Godhead, just as an apple has one essence and existence but different qualities of taste, smell, and color and form; and as fire has light and warmth, so also

---

[1] *Ibid.*, p. 68a.
[2] *Ibid.*, p. 68.
[3] *Ibid.*, pp. 68a–70b.
[4] *Ibid.*, pp. 72b, 74a. Underscoring is mine.
[5] *Ibid.*, p. 74a.
[6] *Ibid.*, p. 74b.

the Incarnation of the Word is indivisible from the essence of the Father and Spirit... However, the Word became flesh and not the Father and the Spirit.[1]

One further question is asked as to whether Christ is God in human nature or Man in divine nature. Gregory's answer is:

> ...To escape both extremes of Nestorianism—dividing nature against nature—and Eutycheanism, confusing the natures, and to take the right course we say that Christ, according to unmistakable union, with his divine nature is man and with his human nature is God... Therefore, we should not say Christ is only man, or simply God, but... the unity of the two... But against Eutyches to say unmistakably: "Keep the attributes of natures in the unity of the unified essences." Therefore, with the divine nature Christ is man, and with the human nature God. Not by mutation, but by communication; that is, in its union that which was remained what it was and became what it was not.[2]

In conclusion, to Gregory the Incarnation was not a metamorphosis of Deity into humanity, or vice versa, but *it is Deity assuming humanity while continuing in the state of Deity*.[3] Therefore, Christ, as the Son of God and the Son of Man, became "God-in-the-flesh... not a mere man... neither solely God, but God become man."[4] This meant that God became man and man became God, one person, one individual, one character, *one nature*, one will, and one operation, *but all divine*.

Consequently, the passion of Christ is the passion of God. For, when one's body is wounded, we say he is wounded and he suffers. "Likewise, the body of Christ is God. For God is crucified, God suffered."[5]

Thus, Gregory becomes the staunch theologian defining the Cyrillian Monophysitism of the Armenian Church. Against the Arians he asserts the essential divinity of the Word made flesh. Against the Docetists he affirms the actuality of the Incarnation of the Word. Against the Nestorians he insists on the unity of the person and nature of Christ, the Word Incarnate. And to Eutyches he replies that the two natures— the divine and the human—must be kept unconfused.

However, it seems to me that it is here that Gregory of Datev fails us. For, throughout his voluminous book he repudiates Chalcedonianism and the symbol of dual nature. *If* Eutyches was wrong in confusing the natures in Christ, then Chalcedon should be right. Gregory, his predecessors and successors, and the hierarchy of the Armenian Church

---

[1] *Ibid.*, pp. 74b–75a.
[2] *Ibid.*, pp. 75a–76.
[3] Arpee, *A History*, p. 180.
[4] *Ibid.*
[5] Datev, *op. cit.*, p. 74a.

have not been able to perceive this inconsistency. To Gregory and the teachers of the Armenian Church Christ is

> the Word becoming flesh and uniting our nature perfectly with his Deity... in one visible nature... and personality, one Lord, one Son... Lord Jesus Christ one, and his nature one.[1]

And, according to Datev,

> he who denies the unity denies the very existence of Christ, and thus, for sure, denies the faith of Christianity.[2]

C. Monophysitism of the Armenian Liturgy

The Armenian Christians of the pre-Gregorian era must have used the Apostolic and sub-Apostolic forms of worship.[3] However, after the national conversion, St. Gregory adopted the Greek Liturgy.

On the invention of the Armenian alphabet, the Liturgy, with the Scriptures, was translated into Armenian.[4] Through the centuries it has been developed and revised to reach its present form. Father Torossian of New York, whose translation of the Armenian Liturgy will be used for this survey, has the following to say:

> ...the Divine Liturgy, now in use in all the Holy Apostolic Churches of Armenians, is very closely akin to that of St. James, St. Basil, and St. Athanasius. Later, it had been rearranged by Nerses the Great, Patriarch of Armenia, about first part of fifth century; by John Mandagoony, Patriarch of Armenia in sixth century; and again greatly elaborated by Nerses Glayetzi, surnamed the Graceful, Patriarch of Armenia in the twelfth century.[5]

The contents of the liturgy follow the customary pattern of invocations, hymns of vestments, ablutions, the processional, the Creed, the Mass, the Holy Kiss, the Institution, Communion, Intercession, Benediction, and the Dismissal.[6]

Chronologically, liturgy preceded theological definition. Later, theology has influenced and revised the liturgy. Therefore, the Armenian Liturgy is replete with Monophysitic ideas.

The most glaring of these is in the *Trisagion*—the Thrice Holy or the

---

[1] Arpee, *A History*, p. 181.

[2] Datev, *op. cit.*, pp. 75b–76a.

[3] J. Bartlett, "Worship (Christian)," *Encyclopedia of Religion and Ethics*, Vol. XII (1924); Acts 2:42, 47.

[4] Arpee, *A History*, p. 24 f.; Ormanian, *National History*, I, cols. 269–282.

[5] Torossian, *op. cit.*, Preface, p. xxvii; Adeney, *op. cit.*, p. 276.

[6] Torossian, *op. cit.*, *passim*; Bartlett, "Worship (Christian)," *op. cit.*, Vol. XII (1924).

Sanctum, based on Isaiah's vision, as indicated above.[1] It dates from the reign of Theodosius II (ca. 408–450), and reads: "Holy God, Holy and Mighty, Holy and Immortal, have mercy upon us."This is sung in all the liturgical churches, East and West. The Roman Catholics use it on Good Friday.[2]

After the Council of Chalcedon, Peter the Fuller—the Monophysite Patriarch of Antioch (ca. 465–474)—added to the *Trisagion* the Monophysitic phrase "who was crucified for us," which is in the *second person* in Armenian (who *wast* crucified—*vor khachetzar*). Thus the liturgical ascription of the Trisagion was formed to read: "Holy God, Holy and Mighty, Holy and Immortal, who *wast* crucified for us, have mercy upon us."[3]

The Armenian Church uses this phrase in its worship, repeated and sung thrice by the choir and the congregation. The Monophysitic phrase "who wast crucified for us" is replaced by other appropriate phrases according to the Dominical feast that is celebrated—such as on Easter: "who didst rise from the dead;" on Annunciation, Nativity, and Epiphany: "who wast born and manifested for us," and so forth. The particular phrase of Peter the Fuller is used on all the festivals of the Saints, the Holy Cross, and the Church.[4]

This phrase seems to have been adopted by the Armenian Synod at Tevin in 551 A.D.—which Adeney gives, erroneously, as 535 A.D.—when the feasts of the Nativity and Epiphany were unified and the Armenian ecclesiastical calendar adopted.[5]

The Monophysitic character of this liturgical ascription is quite evident. It is the "Holy God, Holy and Mighty, Holy and Immortal," who did come and is to come, who was born and manifested, who was crucified and rose from the dead.

The theological controversy known as "Patripassianism" or "Theopassianism"—meaning the suffering of the Father—centered around this phrase of Peter the Fuller.[6]

The Armenian Church—by its adherence to Peter the Fuller's phrase —was involved in the controversy. Gregory of Datev had explicitly

---

[1] See *supra*, pp. 17, 18, 19.

[2] S. S. Cohon, "Trisagion," *An Encyclopedia of Religion. Used by permission.*

[3] Torossian, *op. cit.*, p. 236; Adeney, *op. cit.*, p. 110.

[4] Torossian, *op. cit.*, p. 236.

[5] Ormanian, *National History*, I, col. 544; Arpee, *A History*, p. 128 f.; Adeney, *op. cit.*, p. 544. Adeney conflicts with modern Armenian writers as to the date of the Synod where the Armenian calendar was adopted.

[6] *Ibid.*, p. 110.

said that "the body of Christ is God."[1] "Whatsoever the Father doeth, these same the Son also doeth."[2] Therefore, Christ's passion is the passion of the Father.

Many quarrels, feuds, and fist fights occurred during the controversies around this phrase. In all the negotiations for reunion the Armenians were required to omit the "Patripassian" phrase from the *Trisagion*.[3]

The *ascriptions of the prayers* of the Armenian Liturgy further prove the Monophysitism of the Armenian Church. To take just a few of these will suffice. The celebrant of the Mass, asking for spiritual blessings, prays:

> O Thou, our Lord Jesus Christ, who art wearing the light as thy garment, *and* in untold humility didst appear on earth and walk around with men; who wast made eternal "high priest after the order of Melchisedec" and didst adorn Thy holy Church:
> Almighty Lord, who conferred upon us *the privilege of* wearing the same celestial vestment, make me,... worthy at this hour, as I venture to approach to perform the same spiritual ministry of thy glory, that I may take off all mine impiety,... Grant me to enter with priestly glory upon the ministry of Thy holy things,... So that I also be found ready... to glorify Thee, O Christ, who didst bear the sins of all.
> For Thou art the sanctity of our persons; and to Thee, *our* beneficent God, are becoming glory, power, and honor;...[4]

Here Christ is addressed as "Almighty God" and "Our beneficent God."

Again, on "ordinary Sundays," the celebrant prays:

> O Thou, Only begotten Son, and Word God, and Immortal Being, who didst take upon Thyself to become incarnate from the Holy Birthgiver of God and ever virgin. O Christ our God, Thou, who are unchangeable yet didst become very man, wast crucified, and by Thy death didst trample upon death; Thou being one of the Holy Trinity, co-equal in glory with the Father and with the Holy Ghost, sustain us.[5]

Or again, Christ is addressed:

> ...O Thou ineffable Word of the Father, Thou didst become man and didst appear as our High Priest.
> And as Lord of all Thou didst commit unto us the priesthood of this service and bloodless sacrifice;

[1] Datev, *op. cit.*, pp. 72b, 74a.
[2] Arpee, *A History*, p. 181, quoting Datev.
[3] Adeney, *op. cit.*, p. 114; Der-Nersessian, *op. cit.*, p. 47; Lynch, *op. cit.*, I, 314 n.; Supra, p. 18f.
[4] Torossian, *op. cit.*, pp. 227–228.
[5] *Ibid.*, pp. 235a, 236a.

> For Thou art the Lord our God, who rulest over such as are of heaven and such as are of earth; who sittest on the cherubic throne, O Thou the Lord of Seraphim and King of Israel;...
>
> I beseech Thee,... to... cleanse my soul and mind from all defilement of the evil... And enable me... to stand before Thy Holy Table, and consecrate Thine immaculate Body and Thy precious Blood. . . . .
>
> Inasmuch as Thou art He, that offereth and is offered, that receiveth and giveth, O Christ our God, to Thee we offer glory with Thy Father without beginning...[1]

In this prayer Christ is addressed as the ineffable Word of the Father, "become man, and... as our High Priest and as Lord of all Thou didst commit unto us the priesthood..."

Lastly, the Deacon recites the exhortation:

> And again with faith and holiness, let us stand in prayer before this Holy table of God;[2]
>
> . . . .
>
> Our God and our Lord hath appeared to us . . . .
> We thank Thee, O Christ, our God, who hast granted us such taste of Thy goodness.
>
> . . . .
>
> Preserve us in peace, O Christ our God, under the protection of Thine Holy and venerable Cross: save us from *our* enemies, visible and invisible.[3]

In these last prayers the Communion table is the "table of God"; "Christ, our God" hath appeared; and the "Holy and venerable Cross" is "Thine—O Christ our God."

These prayers addressed to Jesus Christ as "our God" would be quite orthodox *if* addressed only as member of the Trinity. But it is not so; the ascriptions refer to his earthly career as well as to the Son in the Trinity. For, as "Almighty Lord" and "beneficent God" He is "unchangeable yet didst become very man and was crucified." He is the "ineffable Word of the Father... become man," who is "the Lord our God who rulest over... heaven and earth"; "the Lord God of Hosts... who didst appoint us to the ministry"... "one that offereth and is offered ...Christ our God."

These quotations from the Armenian Liturgy illustrate the Monophysitic concepts expressed through worship and prayer, comparable to what John of Otzun and Gregory of Datev did in intellectual and theological definition and formulation.

---

[1] *Ibid.*, p. 240.
[2] *Ibid.*, p. 241a–b.
[3] *Ibid.*, pp. 251a–b, 252b.

D. The Weakness of the Armenian Christology

The weakness of the Armenian Christology is the weakness of the general Monophysite position. The Armenian Church had adopted the Nicene creed, affirming the consubstantiality of the Son with the Father; and the Constantinopolitan creed, confessing the consubstantiality of the Spirit with the Father and the Son. However, the Armenians, with the Greeks, rejected the "Filioque" phrase which the Western (Roman) Church had added to the Constantinopolitan definition of the consubstantiality of the Spirit, specifying that the Holy Spirit "proceedeth from the Father *and the Son*." This fateful phrase was to become one of the major causes of the final break of the Eastern Orthodox Church with the Western (Roman Catholic) Church in 1054 A.D.[1]

The Armenian Church had adhered to the Ephesian canons defining the *unity of the person of Christ*, as opposed to Nestorian dual personality of Christ.

However, the rejection of Chalcedon by the Armenians was anomalous and inconsistent. Chalcedon and the Armenian Church had formally anathematized Eutyches who was the opponent of the Cyrillian "one nature" formula with some exaggeration. Yet, at the same time, Armenians refused to accept the two-nature definition by Chalcedon. While trying to avoid the dualism of Nestorius, they swung to the opposite extreme of so unifying Christ that his humanity remained impersonal—without a rational spirit.

This was not simply an academic error. It was basic for the divine redemption of mankind. Incarnation was the historical revelation of God in a human life. Yet, Jesus of Nazareth, by complete and continual obedience to God, had manifested in himself the perfect creative freedom and love of God. Thus, his will and self-assertion were the "free assertion of God's will" (Dean White). This was due to God's coming to Jesus and his response to Him. Thereby, the broken relation of God and man was restored to an unbroken fellowship of the Father and the Son. Therefore, Jesus "not being in need of redemption himself became the Redeemer" (White).

The Monophysites, while preserving the divinely wrought redemp-

---

[1] Raab, *op. cit.*, p. 10; Ayer, *op. cit.*, p. 305; Percival, *op. cit.*, p. 164; F. W. Buckler, "Filioque," *An Encyclopedia of Religion*; Arpee, *A History*, p. 151; L. P. Qualben, *A History of the Christian Church* (New York: Thomas Nelson and Sons, 1942), p. 149, n. 12.

tion, were destroying the essential element of its accomplishment in and through a truly and fully human person, complete in body, soul, and spirit—Jesus of Nazareth, the Christ of God.

Chalcedon did not provide a modern or complete definition, yet it preserved this basic human element in the divine redemption. For, God is spirit. Man also is spirit, bearing the divine image and likeness. This spirit is transcendent, free, and creative. Spirit knows and recognizes another spirit "by an act of faith, by co-inherence. (White)." This knowledge is immediate. In it two spirits can be within each other, which means personal relationship realized inwardly, without the loss of personal identity. Jesus of Nazareth had this personal relationship with God, and, therefore, he was the perfect son of man.

This perfection was realized by Jesus through his response of faith, love, and obedience to God. "The one God dwelt in him in holiness and power and complete objective reality. He was perfect son, the only-begotten Son, full of grace and truth" (White). And this was accomplished by "the complete co-inherence of the divine and the human persons in each other."

> Not two natures united in one person... nor the divine person displacing the human... but two persons united in one life, one historic existence. (White).[1]

The Armenians, with the other Monophysites, by rejecting Chalcedon had made the redemption a unilateral transaction—God acting in and on behalf of man. Jesus was no more a brother, "in all points tempted like as we are." He was "our God" walking on earth in full, regal dignity and authority. He was born as God, forgave as God, died as God, arose as God, and conquered sin as God. Therefore, he was no more an example, He could not be our model for strength and courage to fight human temptation and sin, for he did so as "our God."

Unfortunately, the Monophysites as a whole thus depersonalized and almost dehumanized Christ. By this they removed him to a distance from mankind, to be worshipped and adored, but not approached as companion in daily life. This attitude, naturally, reflected on the religious life of the Armenians and on their relations with the Muslim environment.

Lately, an encouraging trend is observed among the younger members of the Armenian hierarchy and laity to discuss the doctrinal position of the Armenian Church. Bishop Tiran and Miss Der-Nersessian,

---

[1] Classroom lectures by Hugh Vernon White, Pacific School of Religion, Berkeley, Calif.

both of New York; Rev. L. Arpee, of Illinois, and Bishop A. Poladian, of Antilyas, have discussed the problem. We have already noted the interpretation of Miss Der-Nersessian who has concluded that John of Otzun was a believer in the dual nature of Christ.[1]

Bishop Tiran, too, has tried to justify the Monophysite doctrine of the Armenian Church. He claims that Christ had not only two natures, but even seven—chemical, vegetal, animal, rational, spiritual, angelic, and the divine—but that this last nature, the divine, was "the ultimate and the most comprehensive one dominating and enveloping the lower natures."[2]

It is precisely here that the Armenian Church, with the other Monophysites, is Apollinarian, for according to their teaching the divine nature in the Divine Son "dominates and envelopes" all the rest, including his "rational nature."

The second error of Bishop Tiran rests in his interpretation of the one person in Christ. He claims that Monophysitism rejects "any kind of synthesis in Christ.

> In Christ there are no two beings (as God and man are), nor is he a composition of two beings; hence he is in one nature... The human aspect of Christ's being is assumed by economy... Christ acted... absolutely perfect manhood... He had... acted manhood by economy.[3]

Here the word "acted" is significant. An actor *assumes* the rôle of another person without being that person. So Christ "acted manhood", "he assumed the *form* of manhood according to St. Paul."[4]

So, when the Monophysites speak of the one person,

> they speak... of the one concrete, substantial reality of Christ,... one subject,... one being, the Son, having one set of qualities forming his one nature, including his temporary corporeality in its physical sense.[5]

Thus, all contentions to the contrary, the Armenian conception of the person of Christ is that of divinity with one set of qualities, and the one person of Christ is the subject which expresses these qualities which are divine. His humanity is a mode of activity, a matter of classifying his activities.[6] In essence he remains divine, because the one

---

[1] *Supra*, p. 45.
[2] Tiran, *op. cit.*, p. 12. *Used by permission.*
[3] *Ibid.*, pp. 12, 13–14, 15, 11.
[4] *Ibid.*, p. 15.
[5] *Ibid.*, pp. 15, 16.
[6] *Ibid.*, p. 15.

nature confessed is the divine. It "dominates and envelopes" all else in Christ who has "one set of qualities" as one subject.[1]

In other words, the one person of the Incarnate Word, one subject, one set of qualities, and one nature, are all the divine.

But, nature is the essential qualities of the person of any individual subject. If Christ possessed only one set of qualities and one nature which were divine, where were the human qualities of the Christ? If they were in his *body*, or even the soul—the seat of human life—they do not constitute the person. The person is the spiritual subject, self-conscious, creative, and free.

The natural corollary of this error is readily admitted by Bishop Tiran,

> That our Lord's body was incorruptible, that Christ being sinless, his body could not be affected by the consequences of sin; any fleshly weakness in our Lord as well as any idea of unreality of his body have been repudiated.[2]

This last statement renders the doctrine of the Incarnation quite artificial and irrelevant, for without fleshly weakness there can be no human body. If no weakness can be ascribed to the body of Christ, or if it was not liable and susceptible to any weakness, then it was not truly a human body; therefore the Incarnation was unreal. On the error of Monophysitism Bishop Tiran would be adding that of Docetism.

As many others, Bishop Tiran also feels that Chalcedon did not solve all dogmatic problems, and posits the principle that we should begin the interpretation of the person of Christ with the doctrine of the Trinity, since, he claims, it was fully "fixed beyond all cavil."[3]

However, he forgets that the Chalcedonian controversy was the continuation of the definition of the person of Christ who is the center and core of all Christian dogma. Therefore, without the help of the Chalcedonian symbol, the relation of Christ the Incarnate Word to the doctrine of the Trinity would remain even more mysterious and obscure. Consequently, for a sound doctrine of the Trinity and a sound theology we need a sound Christology.

---

[1] *Supra,* p. 55.
[2] Tiran, *op. cit.,* p. 19.
[3] *Ibid.,* p. 22.

PART THREE

CHRISTOLOGY AND EVANGELISM

CHAPTER FOUR

MONOPHYSITISM AND THE MISSIONARY SPIRIT OF THE ARMENIAN APOSTOLIC CHURCH

We have surveyed, briefly, the history of ecclesiastical relations and the development of the Christology of the Armenian people and their Church. The last chapter was concluded with the statement that the Monophysite Christology of the Armenian Church reflected on the religious life of the Armenians as well as on their relations with the Muslim environment.

We shall now try to indicate the relevance of the Christology of the Armenian Church to its failure to evangelize the Muslim environment with which the Armenian people and the Church were in contact for thirteen centuries. And, to evaluate the problem rightly, we must first briefly review the original missionary spirit of the Armenian Church and the relation of Monophysitism to it.

A. THE MISSIONARY SPIRIT OF THE EARLY ARMENIAN CHURCH

As all churches, the Armenian Church was born of the missionary efforts of the early Christians. Repeated references have been made to the Armenian tradition that St. Thaddaeus and St. Bartholomew preached in Armenia long before St. Gregory.[1] It has been stated also that the legend of King Abgarus (Apkar) and his correspondence with Christ are part of the Armenian national traditions.[2] Finally, as stated before, the national conversion of Armenia to Christianity occurred under Tiridates III with the leadership of St. Gregory, later renowned as "the Illuminator."[3]

St. Gregory was the missionary to as well as of the Armenians. He had preached the Gospel to the Georgians, Albanians, Persians, and Assyrians.[4] The Albanian king, Urnair, received Christian baptism at his hand. On the death of the king, the Albanians asked that St. Gre-

---

[1] Eusebius, *op. cit.*, pp. 59–73; Kidd, *op. cit.*, pp. 428–431; Khorene, *op. cit.*, pp. 106, 110–12, 295.

[2] *Ibid.*, p. 106; Ormanian, *History*, I, col. 22.

[3] Sozomenus, "Ecclesiastical History," *The Nicene and Post-Nicene Fathers*, II, 264.

[4] Khorene, *op. cit.*, pp. 168, 170.

gory's son Gregoris, only twenty years of age, be appointed as their bishop.

Gregoris, with other Armenian disciples trained by himself, travelled and preached in Albania for eighteen years. Then, he preached to the wild tribes of the Huns beyond Caucasus.[1]

The Huns received him warmly. Their king, Sanessan, of the Arsacid dynasty, seemed much interested, but the moral teachings of the Gospel against looting and murder were suspected as an Armenian plot to enable them to live in peace and quiet. Thereupon, Gregoris was dragged to death, tied to the tail of a horse let loose in the steppes of the Caspian plains. His disciples gathered the remains in Amaras.[2]

Yet, Gregoris' labors were not in vain. During the War of Vartan (ca. 451), many Huns came to the help of the Armenians against Persia. Also, toward the end of the fifth century a bishop by the name of Jonas is mentioned to be serving in the land of the Huns.[3]

A disciple of St. Gregory, Daniel the Assyrian, preached the Christian Gospel to the Persians. Sozomenus testifies that the King of Georgia (Iberia) was converted through an Armenian slave woman—named Noune by the Armenian historians—who had fallen in their hands during the era of St. Gregory.[4]

Among St. Gregory's successors, Nerses the Great is noteworthy for his achievements. With benevolent and educational activities, he undertook evangelistic trips and with his colleagues Shalita, Epiphanes, and Gind Selgoony preached to the pagans in the surrounding countries.[5]

One of Nerses' disciples—named the Elder Zwitha, a convert from Judaism—preached Christianity to his fellow Jews and was martyred at the hands of Sapor II of Persia.[6]

Mesrop of Mashdotz was the second great missionary of the Armenian Church. After formulating the Armenian alphabet (ca. 403), he designed one for the neighboring Iberians and Albanians, to enlighten them with the light of the Scriptures which the Armenians were now enjoying.[7] As the result of this missionary enterprise, the Catholici of the Albanian Church were appointed and consecrated by the Armenian Catholicos until the Albanian Church secured its autonomy in

---

[1] Mingana, *op. cit.*, p. 9, note 3.
[2] Faustus, *op. cit.*, p. 13; Khorene, *op. cit.*, p. 189.
[3] Mingana, *op. cit.*, p. 8 f.
[4] Sozomenus, *op. cit.*, pp. 263 ff.
[5] Langlois, *op. cit.*, I, 224, 292; Faustus, *op. cit.*, chaps. XIV, XXVI.
[6] *Ibid.*, pp. 178–180; Khorene, *op. cit.*, p. 470.
[7] Arpee, *A History*, pp. 24–43.

the seventh century.[1] However, the Albanians also assisted the Armenians in their war against Persia in 451 A.D.

Tradition also reports the legend of Mesrop's disciples preaching to the Scythians and converting some of their commanders.[2]

In the sixth century, a bishop and three priests set out to evangelize the Huns. They spent seven years among them, translated the Bible into the Hunnish tongue, and won converts to Christianity. Another Armenian bishop continued their labor and "built... brick churches, planted trees, and various seeds" and "taught those Christian Turks (Huns) how to plant vegetables and sow corn."[3]

In the year 681 A.D., when the prince of the Albanians, Juansher, was assassinated and the Huns attacked them to avenge the assassination of the son-in-law of their king, a bishop by the name of Israel was sent to Varachan, the capital of the Huns, where he preached the Christian faith, converting their king Ilithver to the new religion. In the year 691 two princes were sent to request the appointment of Israel as their permanent pastor, but he was too valuable to be spared. The opportunity was missed and the Huns turned to Judaism.[4]

Hereafter, the Armenian Church is almost altogether silent about evangelism. We read of some correspondence between an Arab poet— Manouche—and Gregory Makistros, who told the entire story of the divine self-revelation in couplet form and forwarded it to Manouche, ca. 1045.[5] However, we have no record as to the effect of this preaching through poetry. Also, we hear of Nerses the Graceful conducting correspondence with some Muslims and sun-worshippers of Mesopotamia, endeavoring to win them to the Christian faith (ca. 1166–1173).[6]

The last noteworthy missionary effort of the Armenian Christians was that of King Hetum I (Haithon) of Cilicia. During his political visit to the great Mangu Khan of Mongolia (ca. 1252–1253), he testified to the Khan and his people about Jesus Christ and his redemption, urging them to declare themselves Christian. The Khan promised him to consider the matter with his advisers. In the meantime, by a treaty he granted protection and freedom to the Christians in his empire.[7]

---

[1] Ormanian, *History*, I, cols. 623 f., 637 f.

[2] Y. S. Kassouny, *The Missionary Spirit in the Armenian Church* (Aleppo: Bozoklian Press, 1940), p. 11.

[3] *Ibid.*, p. 15; Mingana, *op. cit.*, p. 10.

[4] Kassouny, *op. cit.*, p. 15, 16.

[5] Krikor (Gregory) Makistros, *Versifications of Krikor Makistros of Bahlav* (Venice: St. Lazare Press, 1868), *passim*.

[6] Kassouny, *Missionary Spirit*, p. 17; Ormanian, *History*, II, col. 1647.

[7] *Ibid.*; Arpee, *A History*, p. 151; Browne, *op. cit.*, pp. 147, 149, 165–167.

On his return to Cilicia, Hetum and Catholicos Constantine I (ca. 1221–1267) sent Vartan the linguist as their emissary. At this time the Church of Rome appointed missionaries to Mongolia. All of these efforts seem to have been futile, for within half a century the Great Khan's Empire turned to Islam and embraced it officially.[1] Thereafter, the Churches of the East had to fight for their existence.

Before long the Tartars and the Egyptians invaded the last remnant of the Armenian kingdom in Cilicia. Now the Armenian Church had to withdraw into its own shell and devise means and methods to preserve and inspire the faith of its people. From then on the story is one of perpetual conflict, compromise, persecution, martyrdom, and lethargy.[2]

B. The Causes of the Decline of the Missionary Spirit of the Armenian Church

It is very vital for our thesis to examine the causes of this decline in missionary zeal.

Rev. Y. Kassouny, in his pamphlet already quoted, points out six causes of decline, of which he calls three *external* and three *internal*:

1. The fanatical intolerance of the Byzantine Church embittered the Armenians and forced them to hair-splitting definitions and defense of their doctrinal position. This killed the missionary spirit and zeal.

2. The religious policy of the Sassanid Persians forced the Armenians to fight for their faith. Evangelism and war for freedom of religion cannot co-exist.

3. The rise of Islam and its zeal to propagate itself compelled the Armenians to self-isolation, containment, and self-defense. Anxious to preserve national identity, the Armenian Church was unwilling to risk it for evangelism.[3]

Among the *internal* causes of decline, he mentions:

1. The extreme nationalization of the Armenian Church preserved the Armenian national identity but sacrificed the principle of evangelism and expansion.

2. The ceremonialism of the Armenian Church smothered its missionary spirit.

3. The sacerdotalism of the Armenian hierarchy restricted the re-

---

[1] *Ibid.*, pp. 169–171; C. R. Beazley, "Missions (Christian, Early & Medieval)," *Encyclopedia of Religion and Ethics*, V. 8 (1924).

[2] Browne, *op. cit.*, pp. 159, 165.

[3] Kassouny, *The Missionary Spirit*, pp. 19–23.

ligious activities of the laity. Therefore, while the institution was fossilizing and its evangelistic zeal dying, the heretical sects were spreading their teachings—such as the Paulicians.[1]

While all of these causes are historically valid, we should look for the basic answer to our problem: Why was the Byzantine Church antagonistic and inimical to the Armenian Church? Why did the preaching zeal of Gregory, Nerses, and Mesrop not survive to continue the evangelization of the Sassanid Persians, pagan Arabs, and Muslim Saracens? Why did the Armenian Church become extremely nationalistic, ceremonialistic, and sacerdotalistic?

No single cause would be sufficient and strong enough to explain satisfactorily the events and fortunes of fifteen hundred years of Armenian Christianity. Nationalism, racial characteristics, political rivalries of empires, and ecclesiastical jealousies have all done their part in weakening the missionary zeal of the Armenian Church. The Monophysite Christology of the Church of Armenia is *another fundamental cause* which runs through the forementioned causes like a red thread.

C. Monophysitism and Evangelism

When the hierarchy of the Armenian Church and its constituency threw their lot with the Cyrillian formula of the one divine nature of the Incarnate Word, it meant the exaltation of Christ as God and the impersonalization of his humanity. This made the Incarnation a semireal, incomplete event and an appearance—all the assertions of the Armenian writers to the contrary.

Now, the Armenians were committed to defend their position. They were pre-occupied with defining and proving the truth of the *one divine nature of Christ* rather than *studying* the evangelistic appeal of the Incarnation. In the three basic doctrinal documents surveyed we discover no fundamental missionary interpretation or application of the Christan faith.

Even though not put into words by any one, one wonders if the Monophysite Armenians relied on the Almighty Lord to do what *they* should have been doing.

The bearing of Monophysitism seems to be that God, assuming flesh, continued to act in the quality of Deity. Therefore, Christ-God, or Christ-our-God, was and is almighty. He is able to do what he likes, if he likes, where he likes.

---

[1] *Ibid.*

The influence of this doctrinal concept further has been noted in daily life. Throughout the massacres and deportations one question was raised repeatedly: If God was love and almighty, and if Christ was God, why did he not hear and answer the prayers of the thousands of innocent men, women, and children, to save them from massacres, famine, and pestilence?

Or, again, whenever the challenge of the life and teachings of Christ is presented as a personal call to discipleship, the answer given by most Armenians is: "Christ was divine, he was God, he could live sinlessly and serve. We cannot. We are human."

The implications of this position are evident. Christ was God incarnate with one nature. His body and soul were human, but his inner man, inner nature, his essence, was divine. Therefore, he did what he did as God, not as man.

If Christianity is to be effective among the non-Christians—particularly the Muslims—the interpretation of the Incarnation and Christology has a strong bearing on it. Before the Chalcedonian controversy, the Armenian Church was definitely missionary minded. It evangelized the Georgians, Albanians, and the Huns, as noted above. But, after the stand against Chalcedon and the adoption of the one-nature formula, it seems that the missionary zeal began to wane.

As indicated above, Greek fanaticism, Sassanid imposition, the rise of Islam, nationalism, ceremonialism, and sacerdotalism, *all* have contributed to this loss of the missionary spirit. However, all but two of the above hindrances—the Sassenid imposition of Mazdaism and the rise of Islam—appear, to this writer, to be the consequences of the Armenian Christological position.

We have pointed out the persecutions of the Armenians by the Greeks because of the Monophysitic dissent of the Church of Armenia. The more the Armenians insisted on their anti-Chalcedonian position, the more the Greeks acted fanatically. Fanaticism led to coercion, persecution, and even war. Naturally, a church and its people struggling to guard their religious views and to defend their national existence would be unable to think of evangelism and missionary expansion, not to say anything of the resentments and un-Christian feelings occasioned by mutual enmity. The Monophysitic Christology of the Armenian Church being the target of Greek fanaticism and the cause of ensuing persecutions by them, it appears to have constituted *one* of the basic causes of the death of the missionary spirit and zeal among the Armenians.

As to the relation of Christology to ceremonialism, it has been stated

emphatically that Monophysitism overstressed the divinity and mini-
mized the humanity of Jesus Christ. Consequently, in the Armenian
Church the human life and example of Jesus seem neglected and his
divine nature mostly made the object of attention. Therefore, the
Church, as in the Catholic concept, was looked upon as the storehouse
and channel of divine grace and salvation through the sacraments work-
ing *ex opere operato*.[1] As in the Greek concept, the Church was tied to an
unchanging past and a changeless doctrine of Christ.[2] Consequently,
as in all sacramental churches, liturgy and ceremony held the central
place. The Mass, the altar, creeds, and sacraments were emphasized
rather than *personal regeneration, scriptural preaching, Christian service,
and the missionary task*. Thus, on the one hand, leading to self-centered
isolationism, Monophysitism contributed to the neglect of Christian
service and missionary endeavor. On the other, sacramentarian emphasis on the divine nature in Christ and the efficacy of the symbols neglected the *personal relationship* of the believer to the historical and human
Jesus and the apostolic commission to witness to him. Therefore, the
outcome was the abatement and eventual disappearance of the missionary spirit of the Armenian Church. Furthermore, forgetting its missionary obligation, the primary concern of the Armenian Church resolved
itself into protecting its doctrinal identity. No church primarily concerned with its doctrine and unchanging creed can think of missionary
task and obligation.

Again, in a sacramentarian church, the clergy become a distinct
class,

> a priestly caste, divinely set apart for the administration of this trust,
> both of truth and of grace.[3]

Thus, an informal ministry "in time assumes *sacerdotal* character."[4] This
was true of the Armenian Church also.

When Monophysitism isolated the Church, the chief concern of the
hierarchy was to preserve the institution, its mysterious sacraments and
doctrine.[5] The lay people were discouraged and prohibited from
preaching and expressing their religious experiences of the Christian
faith. The interpretation of the Christian heritage, the Scriptures,
Sacraments, and their administration, remained the monopoly of the

---

[1] William Adams Brown, *Christian Theology in Outline* (New York: Charles
Scribner's Sons, 1906), p. 66.

[2] *Ibid.*, p. 62.

[3] *Ibid.*, p. 66; used by permisson.

[4] *Ibid.*, p. 61.

[5] Torossian, *op. cit.*, p. 233.

clergy. Thereby, the Armenian Church, already isolated and distinguished from the neighboring churches by its Monophysite doctrine,
was faithfully and ardently protected by its sacerdotal clergy. And the
clergy, instead of leading the Church and its constituency into the paths
of Christian service and missionary activity, made its basic task the
preservation of the Armenian Church by preserving its Monophysitic
doctrine and separation. Therefore, the duty of going out to preach
the Gospel to all creatures, neglected by the sacerdotal hierarchy, was
performed by the lay members of heretical sects—such as the Paulicians.[1]

As to the extreme nationalization of the Armenian Church, we have
indicated that the Monophysitic break of the Armenians opened wider
the doors of their Church to this influence. As it has been noted heretofore, long before the doctrinal dissension—for over a century—*the
Armenian Church was independent, national, and autocephalous, but in fellowship with the Church of the Empire.*[2] It used the Greek language and Liturgy.
Even *after* the invention of the Armenian alphabet and the creation
of a national literature, the Church was in close communion with the
Church of the majority.[3] But when in 506 A.D., under Papken I, the
Armenian Synod at Tevin repudiated Chalcedon and parted from the
Church of the Empire, the consequent pressure, persecutions, and
attempts at assimilation naturally aroused the national pride, solidarity,
and fervor of the Armenians. And once the breach was complete, the
self-identification of the Church with the interests of the nation seems
to have been the natural course to follow, if not the Christian course.

And when a church is concerned *only* with its own doctrines, the
welfare of its own nation, and the survival of its ecclesiastical and national
identity, there remains little room in that church for missionary consciousness and activity.

Moreover, *with all these causes*, the Armenian Church had *neglected
the core of the essential message* of the Christian faith.

It is incontrovertible that the basic Christian message is the fact that
in the Incarnation God dwelt among us *not* as God "incognito," in
majesty and dignity, but in the flesh, humiliation, in true humanity,
in the person and life of the historical Jesus of Nazareth. Jesus had gone
about doing good, forgiving sins, seeking the lost, and loving to the
uttermost—even to the cross. His last command was to go to the ends

---

[1] Kassouny, *The Missionary Spirit*, p. 22.
[2] *Infra*, Appendix, Diagrams A-D, pp. 136 ff.
[3] *Ibid.*, *supra*, pp. 14, 16, 39 f.

of the world and proclaim to every creature the Good News of the reconciling life and death of Jesus Christ.[1]

The task committed to the disciples was just this—to go to all the world, and be *witnesses* to Jesus. St. Peter at Pentecost, St. Paul in Antioch, St. John in the *Logos* concept, *witnessed* to this one fact—that the Son of God, *Logos*, had become actually human and dwelt among men.[2] St. Athanasius and others fervently defended the fact of the actual, real, perfect, and complete Incarnation.[3]

The Chalcedonian symbol tried to define, however inadequately, the relationship of this unique humanity to the Divine *Logos*, settling on the dual nature formula of the perfect divinity united with perfect humanity. The subsequent "witness" of the Church was that in Jesus of Nazareth there dwelt complete divinity and complete humanity. The Monophysites, and the Armenians, rejected this interpretation.

The Chalcedonian confession proclaimed that God had actually humbled Himself and taken human nature, not as a cloak, or appearance, but actually, truly, completely. God had spoken as Lawgiver, but no one had claimed that He had dwelt fully in a human personality, seeking to save the world. This certainly was "good news" to be published.

But the Monophysites had watered down this unique "good news." Their interpretation of the Incarnation amounted to a kind of theophany. God, in the olden days, had spoken to the Patriarchs in theophany. Now, by the Monophysite definition of the person of Christ, what seems to have happened was that the "theophany" took place in human flesh and continued for a longer duration. God assumed an *acquired* flesh, dwelt *in* human body, but not *as* a completely human person. The real person of Jesus of Nazareth was still God, the eternal *Logos*.

In this doctrine there is nothing particularly and uniquely attractive, specially to Islam. Men already acknowledged God as great, wonderful, majestic, and powerful, but they needed the assurance that He was not *only* these, but also humble and loving, willing to come down to live with men as man. The Monophysites missed *this* emphasis. Therefore, they had no particular message to proclaim to the world of Islam. Theirs was, in a sense, the broadening of the Old Testament revelation, but nothing unique.

What mankind needed was *not* a greater and more impressive theo-

---

[1] H. Kraemer, *The Christian Message in a Non-Christian World* (New York: Harper & Bros., 1947), pp. 73 ff.

[2] Acts 1:8; 2:22–24; 13:23, 30; John 1:1 ff.; I John 1 ff.

[3] St. Athanasius, "On the Incarnation of the Word" (De Incarnatione Verbi Dei), *The Nicene and Post-Nicene Fathers*, IV, 31–67.

phany, but a divine Savior who could identify himself with men; not a subterfuge, but in real fact become man; live, suffer, fight sin and temptation as a man; love and obey God the Father as individual man, wholly, spontaneously, perfectly, uninterruptedly; and thus become the one MAN who could show all men everywhere the IDEAL MANHOOD as intended by God for all, but forfeited by sin and disobedience; and thereby, become the *helper* of men, the Savior of men from disobedience, fear, and distrust.[1]

Metaphysically, Jesus Christ was the *Logos* Incarnate. But metaphysics had not saved Greece, nor had transcendence saved Judaism. Humanity needed a "human" God, a Savior who could truly identify himself with mankind,

> make himself of no reputation, humble himself, and become a servant made in the likeness of men, and obedient unto death.[2]

To sum up, the Monophysite Christology had robbed the Armenian Church of its major evangelistic weapon—namely, the proclamation that God had visited our world to seek and save it, dwelling amongst us as a perfectly human person, yet with a perfectly divine spirit and character.

When we lose this central message of the Incarnation, the truly human person of the Son of Man, there is no vital word for the Muslim environment, where God is already known as a distant potentate to be placated and an arbitrary and whimsical *Allah* to be servilely obeyed and adored, but never to be understood and loved.

Undoubtedly, the steadfastness of the Armenians under persecution and their loyalty to the Christian faith were indirect testimony and light to the Gentiles. However, what the Muslim world needed and still needs is direct and aggressive evangelism.

Had the Armenian Church been willing to go along with the Church of the Empire and to accept the Chalcedonian symbol, it would not have been compelled to take the path of self-isolation and self-defense. Rather, it might have been able to devote its energies to aggressive evangelism and expansion, as in the days of St. Gregory, St. Mesrop, and others; to cooperate with the Church of the Empire in the world wide mission of the Church; and be prepared to evangelize its Muslim environment.

---

[1] D. M. Baillie, *God was in Christ* (London: Faber and Faber, 1948), p. 96; Knudson, *op. cit.*, pp. 318–328 ff.

[2] Philippians 2:6–8.

As history stands, it did not. It chose the path of Monophysitic self-isolation, and, at the cost of blood and martyrdom saved the institution of the Armenian Apostolic Church, but lost the greatest opportunity of direct evangelization of the Muslim Near and Middle East.

CHAPTER FIVE

THE ARMENIAN CHRISTOLOGY AND THE EVANGELIZATION OF ISLAM

The missionary spirit of the Armenian Church and the bearing of Monophysitism on its decline have been briefly considered. We must now inquire more closely into the relation of the Armenian Monophysite Christology to the evangelization of Islam. And, in order to determine rightly the relevance of the doctrine of the Armenian Church to its missionary task among the Muslims, we should first consider the relations of the Armenian Church with its Muslim rulers.

A. THE ARMENIAN CHURCH UNDER MUSLIM ARAB RULE

The first contact of the Armenians with the Muhammadan Arabs took place after the death of Muhammad (ca. 570–632). Persia was defeated at the battle of Kadissiyyeh (Cadesia) in 635 and the entire country was invaded and annexed by the year 643 A.D.

Armenia was entered by Abdur-Rahman (Abdel-Rahman) in 640. His forces penetrated as far as Taron, Pasen, Ararat, and Vaspuragan. The capital city of Tevin was captured on January 6, 641, the day of Armenian Christmas. Catholicos Ezr (Ezras) died during the siege when about 12,000 Armenians were slain and 25,000 captured.

Ever since that fateful Armenian Christmas in 641, the Armenians and their Church have been tossed around like a football between the Muslim Empires on the one hand and the Western Christian Empires on the other.

However, four centuries of Armeno-Arab relations seem to reveal that when the Armenians remained faithful to their word as tributary subjects, generally speaking, their peace was not molested by the Muslim Caliphs. They were oppressed by many individual rulers, to be sure, but this seems to be due more to the personal whims and character of the Arab governors and generals than to the common policy of the Caliphs towards the Christian Armenians.[1]

If, in the reigns of Caliphs Othman (656), Walid (708), Jafar (758), Harun-el-Rashid (786), and Mutawakkil Jafar (839), there were massa-

---

[1] See "The Covenant of Umar," in Tritton, A.S., *The Caliphs and Their nonmuslim Subjects*, (Oxford, 1930) pp. 5–6, *infra*, p. 145; Tabari, *The Book of Religion*, pp. 154 ff. (*infra*, Bibliography, p 145)

cres, persecutions, confiscations, executions, insults, and humiliating restrictions and regulations, and even some forced conversions to Islam, on the other hand, there were long periods of protection and friendly disposition, provided the Armenians were loyal to their word of fealty.

This was the case with Caliph Othman (646–656) until Emperor Constans II jeopardized the safety of the Armenians by reinvading Armenia and forcing the hand of Othman to severity. Or, under Muaviye (661), the Armenians, sick of Greek fanaticism and fickleness, willingly submitted to Muaviye as *dhimmis*—tributary subjects—until Justinian II invaded the land, and, like the Muslims, he himself captured 8,000 souls (688). Naturally, a young and virile state like that of the Muslim Caliphs would not sit back and allow such booty to fall into the hands of the "infidel" *Rums* (Greeks) without struggle.

So also Abdullah was forced to occupy Armenia, but at the urgent plea of a letter in the dead hand of a deceased Catholicos his people were shown mercy by his general, Okba (702). If Walid (708) burned nobles and people in a church, his successor Omar II (717–720) granted the Armenians freedom of conscience and worship and exemption from taxation of church and clergy.

It is fair and morally just to admit that, on the whole, the Muslim Arabs were more generous to the Armenians as tributaries than were the Byzantine Christian rulers. For, when the Armenians were faithful to their word and paid their poll tax—*jizya* in Arabic—they were officially allowed to practice their religious faith without molestation. Whereas, whenever the Armenians were under the Empire rule, almost invariably the question of doctrinal conformity was raised, demanding submission at the risk of persecution.[1] So much so, that Armenians were disheartened, and when Justinian II (688) formally and officially demanded that they renounce their allegiance to Caliph Muaviye and return to the Empire, they answered:

> How often we have submitted to your authority and in our troubles we found no help from you, but, to the contrary, injustice and ravages; if now we submit to your authority again, again we will be betrayed to the sword and captivity of foreign nations, and when you withdraw your hands from us, just as you did at other times, whence shall we find succor? Therefore, we beg you to allow us to remain in our condition.[2]

Do we need to remind ourselves once again of the political as well as the ecclesiastical policies of the Empire? In our historical sketch we

[1] Bury, J. B. *et al.*, *The Cambridge Ancient History*, (Cambridge, 1926), II, 43–46; Der-Nersessian, *op. cit.*, pp. 52 ff.

[2] Der-Movsesian, *op. cit.*, II, 380.

have already seen how many attempts were made to bring the Armenian
Church and its people back to the fold of the Church of the Empire.[1]
The historical record is too clear to be refuted that doctrinal divergence
of the Armenians has been *one* of the major causes of Western coolness
toward Armenian national aspirations and sufferings, even though the
fault of the Armenians themselves must be admitted. To quote a
modern lay writer,

> This charge (of heresy) brought against the Armenian Church by the
> Greek and Latin Churches... was a fertile source of much trouble,
> oppression, persecution, and bloodshed, and almost the sole occasion
> of the overthrow of the last two Armenian dynasties.[2]

As for the Muslim Arabs, their *official* position had been tolerance on
condition of submission and tribute. They had not aimed at assimilating
the Armenians with the Muslims, politically or religiously. The basic
reason for it was in the injunctions of the Prophet Muhammad. He
had sanctioned freedom of worship for the people of the "Book," that
is, the Jews and the Christians, saying:

> Whoever of these believeth in God and the last day, and doeth that
> which is right, shall have their reward with their Lord: fear shall not
> come upon them, neither shall they be grieved.[3]

> Thou wilt find that... the most favourable towards those who have
> believed are those who say, "We are *Nasara*" (Christians).[4]

Unfortunately, however, the Prophet Muhammad was not consistent.
When he failed to convert the Jews and the Christians to his own religious faith, his attitude was changed to bitter enmity towards them:

> And of those who say, "We are Christians," have we accepted the
> covenant. But they *too* have forgotten a part of what they were taught;
> wherefore we have stirred up enmity and hatred among them that shall
> last till the day of the Resurrection; and in the end will God tell them of
> their doings.[5]

This duality has been expressed throughout the history of Islam:
some rulers being friendly, others inimical, to the Christian minorities
and the Armenians.[6]

---

[1] *Supra*, chapter II, pp. 17 ff.

[2] M. C. Gabrielian, *Armenia—A Martyr Nation* (New York: Fleming H. Revell
Co., 1918), p. 109. *Used by permission.*

[3] *Quran*, S. 2:59—*The Koran*, translated from the Arabic by the Rev. J. M. Rodwell M. A. (London: J. M. Dent & Sons Ltd. & New York: E. P. Dutton & Co.,
1918). *All quotations used by express permission of the two publishers.*

[4] *Ibid.*, S. 5:85.

[5] *Ibid.*, S. 5:17.

[6] Der-Movsesian, *op. cit.*, II, 381; Latourette, *op. cit.*, II, 290 ff.; W. A. Shedd,

However, in the centuries-long relations of Muslim Arabs and Armenians, with all the political and national motivations, there was *the silent conflict of religious understanding and conceptions*. A new faith and a united people—Arabs—were proclaiming the unity of *Allah*. They believed in the prophets, revelation, and the sacred books. They accepted Jesus as one of God's prophets and the gospels as revelation given to him. But they held that MUHAMMAD AND THE QURAN WERE THE CROWN OF PROPHECY AND REVELATION.[1]

The Muslim Caliph—as the successor of the Prophet Muhammad—was the vice-gerent of *Allah* on earth and had absolute authority in civil as well as religious matters, so long as he was faithful to the *Quran* and Traditions.[2]

Thus, as defenders of the true faith, Caliphs came into contact with subjects and neighbors of their empire who confessed Jesus to be the Son of God and worshipped Mary as the Mother of God. This idea of the divine sonship of Jesus was an incomprehensible thing, even a blasphemy, to the Muslim mind.[3]

According to the Muslim law, *dhimmis*—the non-Muslim subjects of a Muslim state—were granted the privilege of living, worshipping, and protection in a Muslim country by paying *kharaj* or *jizya*—the tributary capitation tax. Therefore, whenever any Christian minority as the Armenians were entangled in the politics of the Byzantine Empire, they forfeited their right to protection. More seriously, from the *religious standpoint* they were considered infidels and blasphemers. For, by calling Jesus the Son of God, they were giving God a companion—the greatest sin in Islam. Thus, religiously and intellectually, this doc-

Islam and the Oriental Churches (New York: Young People's Missionary Movement, 1908), pp. 96 ff., 150 ff.; Tabari, *op. cit.*, p. 154 f., defends this dual position, saying: "...he who... gives tribute on his hand in an humble condition (Sura 9.29), he spares his blood with this tribute and upon his submission has a right to the compact of protection. If they are averse to tribute and submission, war shall be behind them."

[1] *Fikh Akbar II*, arts. 9 and 16, in *The Muslim Creed, infra*, Bibliography, p. 146; *Quran*, S. 112; 2:256, 285; 4:135; 5:3; 7:158; 25:1; 34:28; 48:24, 29; Al-Ghazali, *Réfutation*, II. 1, p. 9* (Asterisk stands for the text of Al-Ghazali); I. 1, p. 1*; Al-Ghazali, *infra*, Bibliography, p. 144, II; Tabari, *op. cit.*, p. 14 f., gives ten reasons to prove Muhammad's prophetic mission: namely, preaching of One God, character, miracles, prophecies about himself, prophecies on world events, the *Quran*, victories, missionaries, prophecies for him, and his coming last of all.

[2] *Fikh II*, 10; *Wasiyat*, 10, in *The Muslim Creed, op. cit.*; "Khalifah," *A Dictionary of Islam*, 2nd ed.; *Quran*, S. 38:25; 2:28.

[3] Al-Ghazali, *op. cit.*, pp. 38*, 26*; Al-Kindy, *The Apology, passim, infra*, Bibliography, p. 145; *Quran*, 3:40 f.; 4:169; 5:110; 15:29; 19:31.

trine constituted the greatest wall of separation between the Muslims and the Christians, including the Armenians.[1] It is necessary, therefore, to examine at this point the Muslim teaching on the person of Christ.

B. THE MUSLIM CHRISTOLOGY

The central issue between Islam and Christianity is the interpretation of the person of Christ. The misunderstanding of this very fundamental problem has kept the two faiths far apart, persecuting each other in turn.[2] But the doctrine of the person of Christ is inseparable from the doctrines of God and of man. For, ultimately in the Christian revelation both God and man are interpreted in the light of the teachings and life of Christ, and, conversely, the fact of the Incarnation is interpreted in the light of our conception of God and man.

Therefore, to understand and appreciate the Muslim doctrine of Christ, we should inquire into the Muslim teaching on God and man, for on the basis of these fundamental conceptions of Islam Muslims have formulated their doctrine of the person of Christ.

1. *The Muslim Doctrine of God*

The Muslim Creed consists of six basic doctrines: Belief in God, Angels, Holy Books, Prophets, Predestination, and the Last Judgment. Of these, the most central is the doctrine of belief in God—ALLAH— and Muhammad.[3]

To all Muslims, the doctrine of the *unity of Allah* is paramount. "*La ilaha ill'allah*" (There is no God but *Allah*), which is the Muslim "Testimony" (*shahada*), is the foundation of Islam. The essence of *Allah* is will, might, power, force. He is altogether different from man and the world. He is all-powerful, inscrutable, arbitrary, and absolute Lord, even capricious, not bound by his own decrees and decisions.[4]

Thus, God is actually reduced to will—absolute and whimsical. "What pleaseth will God abrogate or confirm," said Muhammad the

---

[1] "Jesus Christ," "Jizyah," "Khalifah," and "Zimmi," *A Dictionary of Islam*; *Quran*, 9:29; 5:76 ff.; Al-Ghazali, *op. cit.*, p. 26*.

[2] M. Ali, *Religion of Islam*, pp. 209 f., 229 note; Tabari, *op. cit.*, 14 ff.; *Quran*, 2:37; 4:48; 5:76 f.; 6:165; 7:140; 3:63; 31:13.

[3] *Fikh II.* 1; *Creed of Al-Ashari*, art. 1, in Klein, *Al-Ibanah*, pp. 31–35 ff., 50 ff., *infra*, Bibliography, p. 144, II; Tabari, *op. cit.*, p. 20 f.; S. M. Zwemer, *Islam, A Challenge to Faith* (New York: Laymen's Missionary Movement, 1907), pp. 86–96; "God," *A Dictionary of Islam*, 2nd ed.

[4] *Fikh II.* 2; Al-Ghazali, *op. cit.*, p. 43*; Klein, *op. cit.*, p. 100 f.; Macdonald, *Muslim Theology*, p. 302; *Quran* 112; 7:52.

Prophet. Therefore, "absolute sovereignty and ruthless omnipotence" are his chief traits.[1]

In spite of the ninety and nine beautiful names given to Him in Tradition, He is a deistic God. God, man, and the world are in exclusive, eternal and external opposition. Being altogether different from all else, the attributes given Him—such as merciful, kind, loving, powerful, creator, watchful, omniscient, are simply human ideas of God, "whereas He may be altogether different."[2]

Therefore, *Allah* in and by Himself is self-sufficient, all-powerful, eternal, and the only Reality. In relation to the creation He is the absolute Knower, creator, sustainer, ruler, destroyer, restorer, exalter, and a baser.[3] In relation to mankind, He is compassionate, merciful, forgiving, kind, guardian, faithful, and patron. He is transcendent and yet anthropomorphic in Muhammad's mind and thought. In later Scholastic Muslim theology *Allah* was separated from His creation altogether. Now He is altogether different from everything else.[4]

The great mystic-theologian of Islam—Al-Ghazali—is well worth quoting at this point. Speaking of God, he says:

> *Allah* is not a body endued with form nor a substance circumscribed with limits or determined by measure. ...Neither is He a substance, nor do substances exist in Him; neither is He an accident, nor do accidents exist in Him... Neither does He exist in anything nor anything exists in Him.[5]

The use of the word "substance" is significant, because, in Islam, "spirit" (*ruh*) is of quasi-material nature and not of "purely spiritual meaning,"[6] Consequently, no Muslim theologian would speak of God as spirit. This is repulsive and abominable to Islam.[7]

The concept of God as almighty will but not spiritual explains the Muslim doctrine of predestination and its corollary the Muslim ethics. God is absolute sovereign and rules by decrees which are eternal and immutable; therefore, "man is necessarily constrained by the force of

---

[1] *Fikh II.* 5; Macdonald, *Muslim Theology*, p. 302; *Wasiyat*, arts. 6, 11, 12, 15; *Fikh II.* 6, 7; *Quran*, 13:39; Zwemer, *op. cit.*, pp. 96 ff.

[2] *Fikh II.* 3; *Quran*, 7:180; Ali, *Religion*, pp. 162 ff.; Levonian, *op. cit.*, pp. 67 ff.

[3] *Quran*, 42:10; 4:164; 2:256; 11:17; 41:14; 51:47, 58; *Wasiyat*, art. 8; Klein, *op. cit.*, pp. 94 ff.

[4] *Fikh II*, art. 2; Sweetman, J. W., *Islam and Christian Theology*, I, 17 ff., 106 ff.; II, 16 ff.; 38 ff.; *infra*, Bibliography, p. 146; Levonian, *op. cit.*, p. 50 ff.

[5] Quoted in "God," *A Dictionary of Islam*, 2nd ed.

[6] Levonian, *op. cit.*, pp. 33, 70.

[7] S. N. Ali, *Teachings of Al-Ghazali*, p. 51, *infra*, Bibliography, p. 146; Macdonald, *Muslim Theology*, pp. 141, 301; *Wasiyat*, art. 8; *Fikh II*, art. 4; Klein, *op. cit.*, p. 83 f.; *Quran*, 17:87; 4:169; 2:81; 16:104.

God's eternal immutable decree to act as he does."[1] This means that God wills both good and evil and that there is no escape from His capricious decrees. His will being certain, arbitrary, irresistible, and inevitable—even before any event transpires—there remains no ground for the idea of a just, righteous, holy, and good God despite the ninety-nine beautiful names for Him.[2]

The Johannine concept of God as spirit might have solved this misconception, provided spirit be interpreted as non-material, actually spiritual personality. This would make God an immaterial and spiritual being in essence and personal; and yet, transcendent as the Muslims hold; immanent as the Muslim *Sufis* (mystics) believe; and non-spatial, dwelling in His creation, as the Muslim creeds profess.[3]

Furthermore, if the Muslim concept of God were revised, the divine attributes would be revised also. Instead of thinking of God as absolute will, power, and omnipotent might—unaccountable to goodness or mercy—He would be conceived as a free spirit, acting freely in accordance with spiritual principles of goodness and love.

But, to the Muslim orthodox believer this is impossible to grasp. In spite of the protest of the rationalistic sects—which believed in human freedom—the day was carried by the orthodox theologians, so that for thirteen centuries the Muslim world has believed in a despotic, unsympathetic, disinterested, arbitrary, and distant God.[4]

The *Shiah* or *Shiites*—followers of Ali—attributed to God physical senses, limbs, and even black hair, but that did not bring Him any nearer. Other unorthodox sects, such as the *Murjiah*—who postponed condemnation of every deed to the Day of Resurrection (Judgment)—ascribed to Him flesh and body in the form of a man, but that created more perplexity until *Asharite* orthodoxy imposed its doctrines on practically all Islam.[5]

We shall soon discover the relevance of this theology to the understanding of the person of Christ and the Incarnation. But we must first review the Muslim conception of man.

---

[1] Zwemer, *Islam*, p. 95; *Quran*, 18:16; 3:80; 2:1, 266, 274; 7:177; 10:26; 28:56; 32:12; 45:22; *Wasiyat*, art. 7; Klein, *op. cit.*, p. 107 f.; Al-Ghazali, *Refutation*, p. 32*.

[2] *Fikh I*, art. 3; *Wasiyat*, art. 6; *Al-Ashari*, art. 5,; Klein, *op. cit.*, pp. 100 f.; 125 f., 128 f.

[3] "Sufi," *A Dictionary of Islam*; Levonian, *op. cit.*, p. 87.

[4] *Al-Ashari*, art. 2; Klein, *op. cit.*, p. 47; Al-Baghdadi, *Moslem Schisms, passim, infra*, Bibliography, p. 144, II; "Al-Ashariyah," "Mutazilah," and "Sects of Islam," *A Dictionary of Islam*.

[5] Elder, *Al-Taftazani, A Commentary*..., Introduction, p. xxiii, *infra*, Bibliography, p. 145; Tritton, *Muslim Theology*, p. 48 f.; Al-Baghdadi, *op. cit.*, I, 1, 5, 6, 129; "Sects of Islam," *A Dictionary of Islam*.

·2. *The Muslim Doctrine of Man*

The *atomistic philosophy* of Islam makes the entire universe to consist of atoms which possess substance and quality. These atoms are created, destroyed, and recreated every moment of time, but in such a rapid succession that the rhythm of creation, destruction, re-creation, re-destruction, *ad infinitum*, gives the semblance of continuity and permanence, whereas every moment everything is created, destroyed, and re-created by the absolute and creative will of *Allah*.[1]

Man is not an exception to this rule. We have already stated that God is *different* from everything else. Therefore, *man is different* from God and is in the same category as the universe and the animal world. God rules man as He rules them. Among the ninety-nine names given to *Allah* are "creator," "maker," "fashioner," and "ruler of all things." The doctrine of atomism provides the principle of the *ground and manner* of creation. The doctrines of the unity of God and the sovereignty of His absolute will imply His arbitrary rule over man and man's helpless passivity as the instrument of the divine decrees and agency.[2] By the theologian and the philosopher God is conceived pantheistically, but to the popular mind He is deistic and aloof. Therefore, the creation is a sample of His arbitrary power and will rather than the manifestation of His wisdom, glory, and love.[3]

Muhammad's declarations on God's creative power are explicit. He says: God "created the heavens and all that is between them in six days... Man hath He created out of a moist germ; yet lo; man is an open caviller."[4]

Thus, God being absolute in and over the creation, man's position and his status in it are obvious. Man is only a worm, made of a sorry germ. "Have we not created you of a sorry germ?... Such is our *power*; and how *powerful* are we! If now ye have any craft try your craft on me," says God through the Prophet.[5]

Muhammad is confused, at times, about man's status. He grants him independence, saying: "Whoso then will, let him take the path of return to his Lord." At the same time, he has man's freedom and dependence as co-existing: "Know ye that... the next life... (is) prepared... for those who believe in God and His apostles." And yet, he goes on

---

[1] Elder, *op. cit.*, Introduction, pp. xxiv-xxv.
[2] *Fikh II*, arts. 2, 5–7.
[3] Zwemer, *op. cit.*, p. 66 f.
[4] *Quran*, 50:37; 41:8; 16:4.
[5] *Ibid.*, 77:20–39.

to say: "No mischance chanceth either on earth or in your own persons, but ere we created them, it was in the Book..."[1]

This confusion of man's dependence and independence is further evidenced in moral wrong:

> If good fortune betide them, they say, "This is from God"; and if evil betide them, they say, "This is from thee." Say: "All is from God." Whatever good betideth thee is from God, and whatever betideth thee of evil is from yourself.[2]

Thus, first man is portrayed as a free agent; later the *Quran* emphasizes his control by God. Even though in the last quotation the source of good is in God and of evil is in man, in Muhammad's mind the author of evil is *Allah*: "I seek refuge in the Lord of the daybreak from the evil He did make," says he.[3]

Consequently, man as created being is devoid of free will, some scant passages of the *Quran* to the contrary.[4]

Not only so, but there is evil purpose in God's creation of man. Men and *Jinns*—genii, i.e., good and evil spirits—are created to suffer and be tortured in hell. "I will surely fill hell with *Djinn* and men together. ...There is not one of you who will not go down to it (hell) that is settled and decided by thy Lord," says God. The most unethical concept of God is in the verse which says: "Thus God misleadeth whom He will, and whom He will He doth guide aright."[5]

Manifestly, Islam sees God as all in all; man is of no significance; he has no rights given him; and he is not free. This is due to Muslim monotheism which is based on pure will rather than reason and love. Hence the sharp contrast of the Muslim doctrine of man with the teaching of the Hebrew-Christian tradition according to which man is created "in the image of God," as a rational creature, endowed with spiritual personality, freedom, and self-determination.[6]

However, to the Hebrews spirit is not the same "spiritual" essence as

---

[1] *Quran*, 78:38–39; 19–22.

[2] *Quran*, 4:81; Tritton, *Muslim Theology*, p. 7.

[3] *Al-Ashari*, art. 5; Guillaume, A., *The Traditions of Islam*, p. 177, *infra*, Bibliography, p. 146, reports this Tradition, which reads: "Bab. None can withhold what God giveth... He that taketh refuge in God from the misery... and... the evil of fate... 'Say: I take refuge in the Lord of the Dawn from the evil He hath created.'" (*Quran*, 113).

[4] *Wasiyat*, arts. 7, 11, 15, 17; *Fikh II*, arts. 22, 29; *Quran*, 113:2; "Perdestination," *A Dictionary of Islam*.

[5] *Quran*, 74:26–34; 72:1; 32:12; 19:72; 88:1–7.

[6] E. Brunner, *Man in Revolt: A Christian Anthropology*, trans. O. Wyon (Philadelphia: The Westminster Press, 1947), pp. 93 ff., *passim*.

the Christian interpretation implies it. In Hebrew thought, man was considered an "animated body," his spirit being quasi-material and penetrating all of a man's possessions.[1] On the other hand, in Greek thought, the soul was considered a pre-existent reality incarnated in man.[2] But the Christian concept of creation is that God creates man free and gives him of His free spirit, a non-material reality.

In Islam, on the contrary, God is absolute and man is a worm in the shackles of pre-destination. The Prophet declares:

> All things have been created after fixed decree (*qadar*)... The Lord hath created... all things, fixed their destinies,... and guided them...
> By no means can aught befall us but what God has destined for us...
> God misleadeth whom He will, and whom He will He guideth.[3]

This misconception of creation and God's relation to man is due to the Muslim misconception of human personality, spirit, and spirituality. As intimated before, in Islam "spirit" is a "*jism*,"—a thing, body, physical. Even God is called a "thing."

The Arabic word for spirit is "*ruh*"—the cognate of the Hebrew word "*ruach*." It is physical, even when applied to God who is called a "thing."[4]

In Islam spirit proceeds from God, takes the form of a man, and brings revelation:

> Say: The Spirit proceedeth at my Lord's command.... with a Spirit... hath He strengthened them.
> Into whom (Mary) we breathed of our Spirit... I have formed him (Adam) and breathed of my Spirit... into him.
> Thus have we sent the Spirit to thee with a revelation...
> And we sent our Spirit to her (Mary) and he took before her the form of a perfect man...[5]

The word *ruh* is used for spirit, soul, and life. It has been defined by a Muslim theologian as

> the nervous fluid or animal spirit. A vaporous substance, which is the principle of vitality and of sensation, and of voluntary motion.[6]

---

[1] "Ruh," *A Dictionary of Islam*, 2nd ed., p. 546b.

[2] Reinhold Niebuhr, *The Nature and Destiny of Man: A Christian Interpretation*, Vol. I, *Human Nature* (Gifford Lectures; New York: Charles Scribner's Sons, 1943), pp. 6 ff.; Levonian, *op. cit.*, p. 25.

[3] *Quran*, 54:49; 87:2; 9:51; 13:30; 14:4.

[4] *Fikh II*, art. 4; Levonian, *op. cit.*, p. 75.

[5] *Quran*, 17:87; 58:23; 21:91; 32:8, 9; 15:29; 38:72; 42:52; 19:17.

[6] *Ibnu'l Asir*, quoted in "Ruh," *A Dictionary of Islam*, 2nd ed.; cf. "Soul," *A Dictionary of Islam*.

Another Muslim author has defined spirit

> as a subtle body, the source of which is the hollow of the corporeal heart, and which diffuses itself into all the other parts of the body by means of the pulsing veins and arteries.[1]

In Muslim thought, *ruh*—spirit—is employed in several senses: Jesus is designated as "*Ruhu-llah*"—spirit of God; it applies to Gabriel; and is used for human life, in which case the source of it is in "the hollow of the corporeal heart." Consequently, its meaning is not that of the human soul or spirit, as we understand it, even though Muslim theologians have attempted to interpret it in this sense. Its true meaning is "wind". *Ruh* in Islam is not a spiritual essence, but non-spiritual, corporeal.[2]

If *ruh* is conceived as material or quasi-material, man would be simply and only a physical and material creature, not spiritual—therefore, not a free being, for in matter there is no freedom. Whereas, Christian psychology and theology maintain that human mind and will are spiritual, transcendent, and free to act.

The mystic theologian, Al-Ghazali, has ascribed to *ruh* immateriality, and accepts a likeness between God and the human spirit, but the Muslim doctrine of "Difference"—*mukhalafa*—of God destroys what he achieves through his mystical insight. For, even to him, ultimately, "nothing is like God, and God is not like anything."[3] Such being the case, there can be no kinship between God and man.

Again, while Al-Ghazali, on the one hand has affirmed the spirituality of God and, inferentially, of man, on the other hand he has spoken of tables and pen being used by God, even though he calls them "spiritual substances." In this the mystic theologian has followed his Prophet who has said:

> We (God) wrote for him (Moses) upon tables of a monition concerning every matter.
>
> The first thing which God created was the Pen (Qalam), and that it wrote down the quantity of every individual thing to be created, all that was and all that will be to all eternity.[4]

The material nature of the spirit can be further deduced from the nature of the *Quran* which one of the famous *Imams*, Abu Hanifah, has called "eternal in essence":

---

[1] *Kitabu't-Tarifat*, quoted in "Ruh," *A Dictionary of Islam*; F. L. Parrish, "Ruah," *An Encyclopedia of Religion*, ed. V. Ferm, 1 vol. (1945); V. Ferm, "Soul," *An Encyclopedia of Religion*.

[2] *Quran*, 4:168; Knudson, *op. cit.*, pp. 93–97.

[3] Macdonald, *Muslim Theology*, pp. 195 ff., 231–232; Levonian, *op. cit.*, 53, *passim*.

[4] *Quran*, 7:142; "Qalam" and "Tables of the Law," *A Dictionary of Islam*.

The *Quran* is the word of God, and is His inspired Word and Revelation... necessary attribute of God ...inseparable from God... sent
down to the lowest heaven complete... revealed by Gabriel... Its
words... writings... letters... verses... meaning (are) arrived at by their
use, but the Word of God is fixed in the essence (*zat*) of God.[1]

Thus, the essence of God is identified with the *Quran*, because "the
Quran is the Word of God" and "the Word of God is fixed in the
essence (*zat*) of God."

In conclusion, spirit being material, there is no relationship or kinship between God and man. Spirits are created by God as stones and
plants are. When the Prophet speaks on behalf of God and says: "I
breathed into him (Adam) my spirit," it does not signify that God gave
of His own spirit to man. "The spirit proceedeth out of the command
of my Lord," said the Prophet. "God neither has spirit, nor is He spirit";
therefore, what man has is not God's spirit, but a creation of God
located in man. Therefore, there is no personal fellowship between God
and man. Man is only a slave (*abd*) of God and Islam is the religion of
servile submission to God.[2]

This leads us back to the core of Muslim difficulty, namely, the problem of the nature of personality and of the interpretation of Reality in
terms of the spiritual personality or physicality. Islam could comprehend human freedom and man's capacity to hold fellowship with God
only by interpreting personality in terms of spirituality. For, as the
Christian faith declares, God is Spirit and man is created in God's image
and likeness as a spiritual personality. Therefore, man is akin to God
in the spiritual qualities of freedom and self-determination as well as
the ethical traits of goodness, truth, and love. Hence the possibility of
communion with God, as advocated by Christianity which has united
God and man in an intimate and personal felllowship. And the Incarnation is its climax. For in Jesus Christ perfect divinity and perfect
humanity have united.

Unless the Muslim world is imparted and is willing to accept this
knowledge of the spirituality of God and man and perceives the fact
of human free will, it will remain enchained by the doctrines of God's
absolute will, relentless predestination, passive acquiescence to fatal-
istic destiny, and the iron hand of immutable divine decrees for good or
for bad, for bliss or for woe.

---

[1] Quoted in "Quran," *A Dictionary of Islam*; *Wasiyat*, art. 9; *Quran*, 80:15; 2:91;
26:193; 53:5.

[2] *Quran*, 15:29; 17:87; 38:72; 2:112; Sweetman, *op. cit.*, II, pp. 183–189; Levonian, *op. cit.*, pp. 74–80.

3. *The Muslim Doctrine of Christ*

The preceding brief exposition of the Muslim doctrines of God and man forces on us the conclusion that for Islam to believe in the Incarnation is an impossibility. If there is no kinship between God and man, God cannot enter history in the life of an historical person. If so, an adequate theology would be ruled out, for "no one knoweth the Father except the Son who is in His bosom." Also, a Christian anthropology would be irrelevant, because the true knowledge of the true man was revealed in the person of the Son of Man in whom God and man were united.

This does not imply, however, that the Muslims did not believe in Christ. The *Quran* is complimentary to the historical Jesus, calling him by the traditional Christian titles—such as Messiah (*Masih*), Word, Prophet, Son of Maryam (Mary), a spirit from *Allah*, Servant of God, and Apostle.[1] Islam believed in the prophets, Jesus being called the Word or Spirit of *Allah*, and Muhammad the Apostle of God, the seal of all the prophets.[2]

Muslims believe in the Virgin Birth and the translation of Jesus to heaven, but reject the crucifixion.[3] They also reject the divine Sonship of Christ.[4]

In Islam there is no need of the Incarnation and the crucifixion, because there is no sense of moral sin or guilt and need of atonement. Every human act, good or bad, is decreed by *Allah*—as seen above.[5] Why should a Muslim feel guilty for his deeds which are preordained and written by the immutable decrees that decide his destiny?[6]

Again, Islam accepted the sinlessness of Jesus with all the prophets, but it considered Muhammad to be superior to him.[7]

Even though Jesus is recognized to be sinless, yet he is not considered to be the eternal Word made flesh. As the Word of God he came into being *after* God gave His creative command "Be":

---

[1] *Quran*, 3:40; "Jesus Christ," *A Dictionary of Islam*; cf. also *Quran*, 3:58; 5:75; 18:109; 4:171; 15:29.

[2] *Quran*, 4:169; 2:130; Tabari, *op. cit.*, pp. 2, 140–8; *Fikh II*, art. 8; M. Ali, *Religion*, pp. 227 ff.; cf. *Quran*, 3:80–84; "Jesus Christ," *A Dictionary of Islam*.

[3] *Quran*, 3:37–43; 19:16 ff.; 57:26; 4:154 ff.; Al-Ghazali, *op. cit.*, p. 32 ff.

[4] *Quran*, 5:76; 19:35 ff.; 3:51; 9:30; 5:19; Sweetman, *op. cit.*, I, 27 ff.; 72 ff.; II, 98 ff.; "Jesus Christ," *A Dictionary of Islam*.

[5] *Supra*, pp. 77–81.

[6] Al-Ghazali, *op. cit.*, Introduction, p. 36 f.; 3* f., 12–13*, 36*, 33*, 46*; Levonian, *op. cit.*, p. 105.

[7] *Quran*, 3:43; 5:112 ff.; *Fikh II*, arts. 8, 9; M. Ali, *Religion*, p. 229; "Jesus Christ," *A Dictionary of Islam*.

> Verily, Jesus is as Adam in the sight of God. He created him of dust: He then said to him, "Be"—and he was.[1]

The Second Coming of Christ is believed in a fantastic manner, expecting him to return to the earth, break the cross, kill the swine, and marry. When he dies he will be buried between the two Caliphs, Abu-Bakr and Umar.[2]

Thus, in spite of the recognition of Jesus as a prophet, he is only in the second heaven with John the Baptist, while Muhammad is in the seventh.[3]

It is obvious that the life and person of Christ have been caricatured by Muslim *Quran* and Tradition.

In Christian theology, the person of Christ is inseparable from the doctrine of the Trinity which is grossly misinterpreted by Islam. This doctrine requires a spiritual conception of God and Christ. Therefore, with its materialistic or corporeal conception of the spirit, personality, and Trinity, Islam can find no room for Christ the Son in the doctrine of God.[4]

We have already noted that Jesus was created, according to Muslim teaching, by the creative word of God —"Be." The plain significance of this is that Christ came into existence at the command of God, and was infused with the created spirit; therefore, Jesus—*Isa*—was not eternal. Consequently, the Incarnation cannot be true, for it means the indwelling of the Eternal God in a historical person. Jesus was a created person, a being; God is different from creation, from any created being, including Jesus (*Isa*). The Incarnation and the Trinity are impossible because there is no kinship between God and man. When God is altogether *Different* or *Other*, how can divinity dwell in a human body and person?[5]

The doctrine of Trinity is known as *shirk*—giving companion to God, the greatest sin in Islam. It is interpreted in physical terms as a tritheism of God, Mary, and Jesus:

> The Messiah, Jesus... is only an apostle of God... Infidels now are they who say, "God is the Messiah, Son of Mary."[6]

---

[1] *Quran*, 3:51.

[2] *Quran*, 4:157; "Jesus Christ," *A Dictionary of Islam*, pp. 234b–235a.

[3] "Heaven," *A Dictionary of Islam*; S. M. Zwemer, *The Moslem Doctrine of God* (New York: Young People's Missionary Movement, 1905), p. 87.

[4] *Quran*, 5:116; 4:171; Al-Ghazali, *op. cit.*, p. 43* f.; Al-Kindy, *op. cit.*, p. 3; Zwemer, *Doctrine*, pp. 85–88; *supra*, pp. 79 ff.

[5] *Quran*, 3:40, 51; 4:168; 19:18; 21:91; Knudson, *op. cit.*, pp. 95 ff.; Levonian, *op. cit.*, pp. 30, 39; Klein, *op. cit.*, p. 67; Al-Ghazali, *op. cit.*, *passim*.

[6] *Quran*, 4:167–170; 5:77, 116; Tabari, *op. cit.*, p. 123; M. Ali, *Religion*, pp. 145 ff.; "Shirk" and "Trinity", *A Dictionary of Islam*.

And when God shall say – "O Jesus, Son of Mary: hast thou said unto mankind – 'Take me and my mother as two Gods beside God?'" He shall say – "Glory be unto Thee! it is not for me to say that which I know to be not the truth;..."[1]

Furthermore, even though the Holy Spirit is referred to by name in the *Quran*, it is not a distinction in the Godhead but refers to the angel Gabriel.[2] In fact, Muslim commentators are said to agree that out of the nineteen references to "spirit" or "Holy Spirit" in the *Quran*, ten are meant for Gabriel.[3]

It is obvious that Muslims—by the very doctrine of Allah—have missed the essence of religion, the meaning of life, and the apprehension of the Incarnation. For to them Christ is *not* THE Word of God. He is only a creature due to the word (*qawl*) "Be" from *Allah*. But the *Quran* is the uncreated Word of *Allah*. Therefore, Islam is and remains the religion of a Book in contrast with the Christian faith which maintains Christ to be the Word made flesh and Christianity as personal surrender to God's Spirit of truth, righteousness, and love.[4]

It is undeniable, therefore, that the doctrine of God has colored the entire field of thought in Islam—its ethics, social organization, religious practice, interpretation of the person of Christ, the Gospel, man, and his destiny. On the other hand, the rejection of the divine Savior— his Incarnation, reconciliation, and redemption—has further darkened the Muslim understanding of God, and caricatured its estimate of man. For, only by turning to Christ we discover God to be a holy and loving Father; man to be a child of God; God a redeeming Saviour seeking mankind through Christ; and His Spirit the ever ready companion indwelling in man's heart to lead him to all truth and to sanctification of his character.

Therefore, all approach to Islam should be made *first* through the living example and spirit of Jesus Christ, rather than the dogmas of the Trinity, infallible Scriptures, divinity of Christ, and the formal doctrine of the Incarnation. Islam does not need more intellectual creeds, of which it has the simplest and holds to it firmly. Muslims need a new power to deliver them from the dark chains of moral sin, arbitrary predestination, and superstition. That power is bestowed in Jesus of

---

[1] *Quran*, 5:116, 117, 76–79; 4:169; "Jesus Christ," *A Dictionary of Islam*.

[2] *Quran*, 16:100–104; 2:81, 91, 254; 66:4; "Holy Spirit" and "Spirit," *A Dictionary of Islam*.

[3] *Quran*, 5:109; 26:193; 70:4; 97:4; 19:17; 2:81, 254; 16:2, 104; M. Ali, *Religion*, pp. 20 ff.

[4] *Wasiyat*, art. 9; Klein, *op. cit.*, pp. 77, 80 ff.

Nazareth whom they respect as the Messiah. Muslims should be convinced that the Christian Gospel is not a matter of mysterious dogmas about "three Gods," but a transforming power for moral and spiritual life.

To summarize, the crux of Muslim error is its doctrine of the person of Christ. Had it understood Christ right, Islam would have had a truer conception of God and a higher evaluation of man.[1]

While in Islam God is conceived as totally different from man and the Incarnation as an impossibility, the Christian conceives God as Holy Love, revealed in Jesus of Nazareth; the spirit of God conferred upon man in *some* measure which was manifested in Jesus Christ in *full* and perfect measure. And this spirit is not a substance, or material thing, but moral personality. Therefore, to the Christian, God is not absolute will, power, and force, but love, truth, and righteousness.

Muslims cannot accept this truth because of their unspiritual interpretation of *ruh*. To them God is not spirit; He creates it. God is so *different* from man that even Jesus of Nazareth cannot bridge the gap, for God cannot be identified with any created being.

If the Muslim mind could be penetrated and communicated the idea of the affinity between God and man, the Christian churches and missions might find the solution to the relationship between Islam and Christianity.

The misinterpretation of *ruh* has resulted in the misconception of the human soul as unspiritual, a body susceptible to death, and man as unfree, because freedom is a spiritual quality. Hence the absolute predestinarian teaching of Islam.[2]

Naturally, absolute predestination has destroyed the sense of ethical responsiblility. God decrees all. Man chooses and acts as Allah decrees, permits, and enables him to choose and act. Obviously, this destroys the whole concept of moral sin and guilt. Even if sin is pride and opposition to *Allah*, He is the author of good as well as evil, for He decrees all. While in Christianity God's freedom is governed by holy love, in Islam divine freedom is arbitrary. Therefore, nothing would be evil or wrong in itself and by nature, as God ordains and allows it.[3] For "God misleadeth whom He will and whom He will He guideth." "By no means can aught befall us but what God has destined for us."[4] For, "when God

---

[1] *Supra*, pp. 77 ff.

[2] *Quran*, 54:49; 14:4; 5:1; Tritton, *Muslim Theology*, p. 171; *supra*, pp. 79 ff.

[3] *Wasiyat*, arts. 7, 11, 15, 17; *Fikh II*, arts. 5–6; E. Sell, "Sin (Muslim)," *Encyclopedia of Religion and Ethics*, XI (1924).

[4] *Quran*, 14:4; 9:51.

createth His servant for Paradise his actions will be deserving of it until he die; when God createth one for the fire, his actions will be like those of the people of hell till he die..."[1] These quotations demonstrate that for the Muslim sin is not "an offense against an immutable moral law of right or wrong," but simply "the neglect of the arbitrary decrees of an absolute Ruler."[2]

This conception of God and sin explains the fact that to Muslims adultery, murder, flight in battle, and the neglect of the daily duties of Islam are equally sinful. In Islam there is no differentiation of *moral failure* from social or ceremonial negligence. In Islam sin is a human weakness and God's abundant mercy its remedy.

Islam is an extremely legalistic system of religion, where there is no "categorical imperative" of love of God "with *all* thy heart, mind, and strength" and man, "thy neighbor, as *thyself*": no sense of *moral* sin and guilt, no sense of *need* of *redemption, atonement,* and *incarnation.*

Such a conception of sin required a similar device of pardon and salvation. Actually, sin is disobedience to the absolute commands of God revealed through the Prophet. Salvation (*najat*), therefore, is not a matter of moral regret, inward transformation, and new life, but forgiveness (*maghfirah*) secured by reciting the creed—*Kalimah*—"There is no God but Allah and Muhammad is His Apostle," and observing the duties of Islam. Thus the discharge of the five practical duties of Islam—the Testimony, five daily prayers, fasting in *Ramadan,* alms-giving, and pilgrimage to Mecca—becomes the key to Salvation or forgiveness.[3]

The *destiny of man,* too, is decreed by God. For the quasi-material soul of man there is provided sensuous pleasures of paradise and physical tortures of hell: physical delights for the obedient Muslim, and bodily torments for the disobedient![4] Everything is based on the physical for lack of a spiritual conception of God and man.

How totally different is the Christian understanding of man, because the Son of Man has revealed the true nature of God and man. Human

---

[1] "Predestination," *A Dictionary of Islam.*

[2] Sell, "Sin (Muslim," *Encyc. of Rel. & Ethics,* XI (1924); J. L. Barton, *The Christian Approach to Islam* (Boston: The Pilgrim Press, 1918), pp. 52–57; Sweetman, *op. cit.,* II, 196 ff., 209 ff.

[3] *Quran,* 53:32, 33; 25:71; 33:71; Sweetman, *op. cit.,* II, 2, 53 ff., 208 ff.; "Pardon," "Repentance," "Salvation," and "Sin," *A Dictionary of Islam.*

[4] *Quran,* 2:22, 23; 76:12–22; 56:12–39; 55:54–56; 47:16, 17; 4:11; 54:47; Levonian, *op. cit.,* p. 89; "Hell," "Paradise," *A Dictionary of Islam;* M. Ali, *Religion,* p. 303 f.; also cf. *Quran,* 101:9; 54:24; 104:4, 5, 6, 7; 57:20; 86:9; 50:22; 2:167; 22:30, 31; 6:71; 20:81; 18:104 ff.

mind unaided is unable to arrive at the ultimate knowledge that God is Spirit and Holy Love, and that man is His child. Mankind needed the revelation of the Incarnation whereby these truths were made manifest. On the reality of them, Jesus of Nazareth risked his life.

How greatly, therefore, Muslims need the illumination of the life and teachings of Jesus Christ. How urgently they need deliverance by him from the false conception of the tyrannous will of *Allah*! How necessary it is for them to comprehend the revelation in Christ that man as child of God is a free agent, and that all law and prophets are fulfilled in the commandment of love to God and love for man!

C. The Armenian Christology and the Evangelization of Islam

This lengthy digression was undertaken to clarify the fundamental concepts of Islam on the nature of God, man, and Christ, in order to determine the implications of the Monophysite Christology of the Armenian Church amidst its Muslim environment.

In our review of the Armenian Christology we arrived at the conclusion that its Monophysitic doctrine deprived the Church of Armenia of its most vital and unique message—that in the Incarnation God was revealed in a truly human personality, perfectly human in body, soul, and spirit, that He might redeem human personality to become Christlike and God-like.[1]

We can see readily the irrelevance and futility of the Monophysite position in face of Islam and its interpretation of the person of Christ.

We have discovered that to Islam God is the *absolutely other than man*. There is no affinity between *Allah* and man. Therefore, the Incarnation is impossible and fictional. *It cannot be.* This was, and still is, what Islam holds concerning the Incarnation and Christ.

On the other hand, the Monophysite formula everywhere confirmed, so to say, what Islam maintained.

The one-nature formula would play into the hands of the Muslim theologians, unwittingly, of course. For, it insisted that although the Incarnation was a fact, the humanity of Jesus was not complete and perfect—the Armenian creed to the contrary, which is based on the Nicene formula. It was an "impersonal humanity." His mind, spirit, was the *Logos*.

Islam already maintained that God could not come into contact with

---

[1] *Supra*, chapter IV, pp. 63 ff.

man, could not be incarnated in humanity, that Jesus was not the Son of God, but only the son of Mary.[1] The Monophysite Christology confirmed this opinion, *negatively*. The official Synods declared, and, inferentially the Liturgy proclaimed in worship and prayer, that God did not, and could not, become *fully* human. He only presented an *appearance* in which the human was deified rather than the divine being *totally* humanized.

This type of Christology would, naturally, blunt the edge of the Christian message to Islam. There is nothing essentially unique to be offered by Monophysitism to the Muslims. What Islam needed was the testimony that God had *truly* dwelt among men in a perfect man—in a simple, ordinary, human life, completely and totally human. This the Armenian Christians could not say because they maintained that there dwelt in the Incarnate Son one *unified nature* which was divine—"one nature of the Incarnate Word."

Again, the Monophysite Christology was irrelevant and ineffective because it appeared to commit the very "sin" which was the greatest of all sins in Muslim theology—namely, the sin of "shirk," giving a companion to God, which was polytheism and idolatry.

If Christ was God "incognito," and was worshiped as "our God," as the theology and liturgy of the Armenian Church amply prove, then the Armenian Christians would seem to the Muslims to be doubly guilty. First, they would seem guilty of thinking of God as Incarnate in a human body, and, secondly, of worshipping that human person as God. In other words, it meant that *the Monophysites were worshipping the form of a man as God*. Obviously, the hair-splitting definitions of Cyril or Eutyches would be incomprehensible to the crudely materialistic mind of Islam which totally and absolutely rejected the idea of any incarnation.[2]

The basic difference between Christianity and Islam was in the persons of Jesus and Muhammad. Muhammad spoke in the *name* of Allah. His character was common knowledge. Jesus of Nazareth, a perfectly human person, also had spoken in the name of the true God. But he had named Him Father, and—as St. John interpreted it—he had identified himself with the Father, saying, "I am in the Father and the Father in me"; "he that hath seen me hath seen the Father"; "I am the way, the truth, and the life."[3] And Muslims admired his life, character, and

---

[1] Al-Ghazali, *op. cit.*, pp. 26*, 32*, 36*.

[2] M. Ali, *Religion*, p. 422; Al-Ghazali, *op. cit., passim*.

[3] John 14:10–11, 9, 6, King James version.

teachings, although they thought the Christians had altered and falsified the gospel records.[1]

However, the Monophysite Christology and interpretation had shorn Christ's humanity of its essential reality. He was conceived as God walking on earth, worshipped in awe and reverence and represented by images and icons, but not approached as a human brother who could teach the true nature of the heavenly Father and of human destiny. He was not approached as the human teacher who was so identified with the spirit, will, and purpose of the Father that God had acted through his life and love.

Islam needed to bridge the gap between almighty *Allah* and man. The doctrine of the Incarnation claimed to have accomplished it, but the Monophysite Christology had artificialized, if not almost annulled, it.

Lastly, the doctrine of the Trinity has constituted the greatest stumbling block to the Muslim mind, both by its metaphysical implications and polytheistic interpretations.[2] In this doctrine Christ holds the central place.

We have remarked more than once that the unity of *Allah* is paramount in Islam, and, therefore, Muslim enmity to "tritheism" implacable. In fact, Muhammad's monotheism was so earnest and absolute that he did not hesitate to command *fighting* against those who held the contrary view.[3] In the conflict between Muslim monotheism and Christian "polytheism"—Trinitarianism—the victory was assured to the former.

The Monophysite Christology would arouse to a greater extent this Muhammadan antagonism to the doctrine of the Trinity. For, here, it was not Christ in glory that was recognized as the Son of God and the Second Person of the Trinity; this the Armenian Church confessed with all others. But also the earthly life of Jesus Christ was considered to be the life of the Eternal Word; the Word of the Father had assumed a human flesh to Himself and was worshipped as Lord and Savior, always remaining as the Word in the form of human flesh. Surely this would invite greater opposition on the part of the Muslim public and theologian.

To the present day, all Christians in Muslim lands—including most of the Western missionaries during the past century and a half—have

---

[1] Tabari, *op. cit.*, p. 150 ff., 13.

[2] Tabari, *op. cit.*, pp. 123 ff., 166 ff.

[3] *Quran*, 9:29–32 ff.

emphasized and re-emphasized the doctrine of the Trinity, the divine Sonship of Christ, and the indwelling of the Holy Spirit, all of which have blocked the approach to Islam.

To us as Christians these are obvious truths of the Gospel, but to the Muslim mind they are riddles, and even blasphemies.[1] The ultra-transcendent conception of God in Islam has led the Muslims to interpret the Trinity in terms of physical relationship of God-Mary-Jesus. And to this, the Christians themselves have fed not a little fuel by actually worshipping Mary as "Mother of God."

Obviously, no Christian church, orthodox or Monophysite, should accommodate its teachings and the Christian message to the false conceptions of Islam. But, the approach should, and, could, have been different. The Muslim mind did not need further emphasis on the mystery of the Godhead by the doctrine of the Trinity, however much true and essential for our faith. To them the *unity* of *Allah* is the heart of true religion. It is such a basic tenet of Islam that one chapter of the *Quran* is entitled "The Unity" and reads: "In the Name of God, the Compassionate, the Merciful."

> Say: He is God alone:
> God the eternal!
> He begetteth not, and He is not begotten;
> And there is none like unto Him.[2]

Muhammad Ali, commenting on this *sura* and the unity of God, says:

> The third verse is plain enough. God cannot be described either as a Father or as a Son as the Christians hold... The fourth verse declares that none is like God, and thus deals a death-blow to such doctrines as those of Incarnation and Manifestation, the latter being the basic doctrine of the Bahai religion.[3]

Further, speaking about the Incarnation, he claims that

> revelation must be communicated through a man... Hence faith in the messengers of God is mentioned along with faith in the revealed books (Sura 2.177, 285)... The prophet is... the bearer of the Divine message... It is the prophet's example that inspires a living faith... This is why the Holy Quran lays special stress on the fact that the prophet must be a man... an angel is sent as a messenger... and cannot serve as a model for men. ...much less would God Himself serve that purpose,... because... man has to face temptations at every step, but there is no temptation for God.[4]

---

[1] Al-Ghazali, *op. cit.*, p. 26*, *passim.*
[2] *Quran*, 112.
[3] M. Ali, *Religion*, p. 422, n. 1. *Used by permission.*
[4] *Ibid.*, pp. 221–222; Tabari, *op. cit.*, p. 20.

It is evident, therefore, that to Muslims God is mysterious enough.[1] What they needed, and still need, is the true understanding of the nature of God, the destiny of man, the nature of moral wrong, and the way of salvation.

The Monophysite or Dyophysite approach of theology, presenting God as a mysterious "Three-in-One" or "One-in-Three" existence, would not appeal to the Muslim mind—as the history of missions in Muslim lands testifies. The real appeal is to be found in the actually human person of Jesus Christ. If God's true nature and man's true destiny are to be made known to Islam, this can be accomplished by a practical approach, based on the truly human personality of Jesus of Nazareth, rather than the dogmatic and theological presentation. The Monophysite definition had misinterpreted and neglected this human approach, while the Dyophysites had materialized and misrepresented it by icons and relics.

The net outcome of the Monophysite Christology vis-à-vis the Muslim theology appears to be that the intellectual avenue of contact between the two faiths was obstructed. National and political entanglements impeded their mutual fraternization and jeopardized the safety of the Armenian Church. An available avenue might have been the intellectual and philosophic approach. But this seems to have been barred by the over-emphasis of the divine nature of Christ, however true and essential it be. The Armenian Christians appear to have ignored the appeal and application of the human life, love, kindness, purity, sincerity, and service of Christ.[2]

Having neglected this aspect of the Christian faith, the Armenian Church—with the others—lost the opportunity of proclaiming to the world of Islam the message that God is a spiritual Father, resembling Jesus of Nazareth in heart and character; that He is not an arbitrary despot, but a loving Father disposed to assist men and women to amend their courses of action; that He does not will evil and wickedness, but holiness and love as manifested by Jesus; that He is not an absentee Lord, but ever-present Father yearning for fellowship with men as Jesus did; that He is not totally different from man, but His image dwells in man as it did perfectly in Jesus; that man is not a worm, but a child of God called to a Christ-like life and cooperation in establishing a kingdom of righteousness as proclaimed by Jesus.[3]

---

[1] *Fikh II*, arts. 2, 4.

[2] A. C. Knudson, *The Doctrine of God* (New York: The Abingdon Press, 1930), pp. 318 ff.

[3] *Ibid.*, pp. 426, 106 ff.

If these truths were imparted to the Muslims, dogmas might have been accepted readily in due time. Now, neither has been accomplished because of the overemphasis of dogma.

It might be asked quite justifiably: If the Monophysite doctrine was one of the major causes of the failure of the Armenian Christians to evangelize Islam, have the Dyophysites succeeded? They have *not* because of the error in the same direction. While doctrinally the Dyophysites have accepted the complete reality and perfection of the human personality of Christ, in practice they seem to have made a false presentation of it by overemphasizing the Trinitarian dogma, stressing Mary as "Mother of God," and idolizing and worshipping Jesus Christ through icons, statues, pictures, crucifixes, and relics.[1] All of these, of course, smacked of idolatry and polytheism to the Muslim mind.

On the other hand, when the humanity of Jesus has been presented in its true light, missions seem to have succeeded better, such as by the Arians and Nestorians,[2] even though these movements arose *before* the Muslim era. It is likely that the Unitarian approach might be more appealing among the Muslims. *Not* that we advocate a unitarian Christology, but that Christology should not be made a stumbling block in our approach to Islam, especially so in the early stages of evangelism in Muslim lands.

As it has been maintained throughout the foregoing pages, the first emphasis should be on the genuine human personality of Jesus Christ, his *perfect* obedience to God, his character, his life of service, and teachings. The question of *whence*, no doubt, would be raised and answered in due time. Of course, the prohibitive law of Muslim lands against conversion has to be reckoned with, but literature and an intellectual approach are convenient channels for reaching them.[3]

---

[1] Adeney, *op. cit.*, pp. 189 ff.

[2] Latourette, *op. cit.*, I, Introduction, p. xviii, 213–215, 230–231, also 195–206, 357; Walker, *op. cit.*, pp. 129–130; J. H. Barrows, *The Christian Conquest of Asia* (New York: Charles Scribner's Sons, 1899), p. 213.

[3] Cf. *infra*, Appendix, Diagram J, p. 140; also, W. A. Shedd, *Islam and the Oriental Churches* (New York: Young People's Missionary Movement, 1908), pp. 223, 224; Richter, *op. cit.*, pp. 85 ff. Both of these two volumes give the traditional, doctrinal approach to the Muslims as used in the past.

PART FOUR

CHRISTOLOGY, NATIONALISM, POLITICS

CHAPTER SIX

ARMENIAN CHRISTOLOGY, NATIONALISM, AND POLITICS

It is no revelation to state that politics have played an important rôle in the life of the Armenian Church. Behind it lay the spirit of nationalism, and in the background of both rested the Christological position of the Church of Armenia.

Throughout this thesis we have tried to demonstrate that the Christological isolation of the Armenian Church contributed greatly to its distinctly national character. Inevitably, the national spirit developed into nationalistic and political aspiration. These came into fierce conflict with the ruling Muslim state, namely, the Ottoman Empire, and the outcome was tragedy.

We have had occasion to state that beginning with the Muhammadan era the fate of the Armenian Church and its people depended on the goodwill and policies of the Muslim Caliphs. Caliph Othman was the first Muslim sovereign to secure the allegiance of the Armenians as a tributary kingdom. Throughout the four centuries of Muslim Arab era and the political rivalries of the times, Armenians and Armenia were in a perpetual see-saw of subservience between the Muslim Caliphs and the Byzantine emperors.

A. Armenians under the Turkish Rule

It was in the year 943 A.D. that the Turks first entered the outlying provinces of Armenia via Persia and Mesopotamia. The large scale invasion of the land of Ararat by the Turks occurred half a century later (ca. 1021) when Toghrul Bey invaded Nakhichevan and Tevin. Ani, the capital city, fell in 1065, and Prince Ruben established the Rubenian Kingdom of Cilicia in ca. 1080. With the fall of Ani, Armenia was overrun and occupied by the Turks.

Some of the salient facts about the relations of Armenians and Turks are:

(1) Ever since the Turks came into contact with the Armenians in the tenth century (943 A.D.) and the fall of the capital city of Ani in 1065, the fate of this Christian nation has been determined more by the personal dispositions of the rulers than solely by Muslim religious in-

tolerance. The Turks have *repeatedly* invaded and pillaged the land of Armenia, capturing and massacring its people. This was not so much to convert them to the Muslim faith as to incapacitate them to resist their military campaigns and depredations in order to fill their treasury by looting this ancient land and its prosperous people.

In other words, the Turks have endeavored to secure a foothold in this very strategic plateau—the highway of empires—just as the Byzantine emperors had striven to do. In this game of power politics, the "Christian" rulers of the Eastern Roman Empire had not invaded or persecuted Armenia *any less* than "Muslim" Persian Shahs, Arab Caliphs, and Turkish Sultans.[1]

Therefore, it seems to be the fact that the earliest incursions of the Seljuk and *Osmanli*—Ottoman—Turks into Armenia, and the consequent massacres, persecutions, and captivities were motivated by political domination and imperialism.

When these political ambitions combined with the rough, wild, Asiatic-Mongolian traits of looting, pillaging, killing—as those of Jengis Khan, Tamerlane, and the Sultans—and with the subsequent fanaticism of Islam, the net result was bloodshed without mercy and domination with an iron hand.[2]

(2) Even this, however, up to the accession of Abdul Hamid II in 1876, was sporadic and punctuated, depending on the personal character and whims of the Turkish Sultans and Arab Caliphs, and the national attitude of the Armenians. So much so, that in spite of the challenging participation of Prince Ruben, of Cilicia, in the campaigns of the First Crusade (1098), within half a century one of his successors could conclude a treaty of friendship with Kludg Arslan of the Sultanate of Iconium (1153). In another century, this friendship was reversed and Hetum entered into a defensive alliance with Baiju Khan of Mongolia against the Sultanate of Iconium, ca. 1256. But Hetum's friendship was rewarded by the capture and slaughter of the King, the Regent, and forty nobles of Cilicia, by Bilarghu, the commander of Tartar forces (ca. 1307).[3]

---

[1] Der-Nersessian, *op. cit.*, pp. 7–8, 13, 14–19, 29 ff.; Arpee, *A History*, pp. 44 ff., 75 ff., 131 ff.

[2] J. L. Barton, *Daybreak in Turkey* (Boston: The Pilgrim Press, 1908), p. 65; E. L. Clark, *The Arabs and the Turks* (Boston: Congregational Publishing Society, 1876), pp. 73–79, 103–110, 122 ff.; E. S. Creasy, *History of the Ottoman Turks* (New York: Henry Holt and Company, 1877), pp. 105–109; Der-Movsesesian, *op. cit.*, II, 425 ff.; Ormanian, *History*, I, cols. 1241 ff.

[3] Ormanian, *History*, II, cols. 1619 ff.; Arpee, *A History*, pp. 155 ff.; Toynbee, *op. cit.*, pp. 617 ff.

When the Karaman Turks invaded Cilicia, Armenians were again assisted by Abu Said Khan and his army of 20,000 against the Egyptians and the Turks. But this was reversed again. Tamerlane, the Great Khan of Mongolia, invaded Armenia as far as Sis, the capital of Cilicia (ca. 1401). Soon, the Turcoman tribes entered the country (ca. 1422–1437), but their rule was terminated abruptly by the hands of the Sufi dynasty of Persia (1502).

If Muhammad II was a fighting successor of the Prophet, he was also wise and friendly enough to grant the Armenians of Constantinople the status of equality with the Greek element. He established the Patriarchate of Constantinople in 1461 and introduced the "millet" system of religious and civil autonomy of the Christian minorities under their respective patriarchs.

It was in the reign of his successor Suleiman the Magnificent that the Janissaries—the army of Christian male children converted to Islam—was instituted; and the Christians, including the Armenians, who opposed the cruelty of the Janissaries were massacred and their churches burned (ca. 1543).[1]

(3) Even in the darkest pages of Armenian history, when Shah Abbas of Persia inflicted one of the severest persecutions of Christians, we find the constructive activities of Moses of Datev, redeeming what Abbas had looted and rebuilding what he had destroyed (ca. 1627).[2]

(4) Furthermore, during the seventeenth century the Armenians of the Turkish Empire had suffered more from the Papist and nationalist factional disputes and the consequent intervention of the Turkish Government than by any systematic Muslim-Turkish persecutions. It is an added shame that these internal family feuds had to be arbitrated by the hands of Muslim Sultans—such as Mustapha II and Ahmed III. It is obvious that the Turkish Sultans encouraged these Christian factions only to "divide and rule." But it was more disgraceful that these Papist versus Armenian nationalist parties fought one another with the connivance of Catholic France on the one hand and the Muslim Turkish Government on the other.[3]

(5) The next century and a half—eighteenth to the middle of the nineteenth—was a period of continuous enlightenment and remarkable progress for the Armenians in Turkey. Churches were rebuilt and repaired under John Golod (ca. 1715); hospitals were established by

---

[1] Ormanian, *History*, II, cols. 2154 ff.; Creasy, *op. cit.*, pp. 11–98.
[2] Ormanian, *History*, II, cols. 2300–2303; Arpee, *A History*, pp. 221 ff.
[3] Arpee, *A History*, pp. 157 ff., 163 ff., 252 ff.

Zecharias of Galzwan (ca. 1773); and schools were founded by Haru-
tune Bezjian (ca. 1832).[1]

One sour note was the confiscation by the Turkish Government of
the silver plates of all the Christian churches (1787–1792). This *might*
have been due as much to the emergencies and financial burdens of the
Austro-Russian war against Turkey and a reprisal against the friends
and sympathizers of the enemy as to Muslim encroachment on the
Christians.[2]

The most significant fact of this period, however, was the reform
movement inaugurated by two Imperial edicts which granted special
rights and privileges to the Christian minorities in general and religious
autonomous status to the Armenians (1839, 1860). If these decrees were
not executed, it was due more to political considerations and the social
advantage of keeping the Christians subservient and inferior than to
religious motives.

We cannot say, therefore, that thus far the Muslim Turks aimed at
the *total* destruction or conversion of the Armenian minority in the
Ottoman Empire.[3]

(6) However, this situation was totally reversed by the accession of
Abdul Hamid II and the rise of the Young Turk Nationalist Party, of
which Midhat Pasha, the minister without portfolio, was the leader.

The internal political reform movement inaugurated by Sultan
Mahmud and his Imperial Edict of 1837 was affirmed by Sultan Abdul
Medjid's edicts of *Hatti Sherif of Gulhane* (1839) and *Hatti Humayun*
(1856), and by the edict of Abdul Aziz (1861). These proclamations were
the messengers of a new day of freedom, equality, and security of life,
honor, and property to the Christian minorities in Turkey. They
demonstrate the efforts of some of the Sultans of Turkey in spite of the
fact that they were at the same time the Caliphs of the Islamic world,
sworn to defend the faith of Islam.

On the basis of this liberalism the Armenians were granted the civil
and religious administrative constitution.[4]

However, the class of *Ulama*—learned doctors in Muhammadan
divinity and law—a religious caste which belonged to the old, fanatical
and conservative, Muslim school of thought, resented the European

---

[1] Arpee, *A History*, pp. 238 ff., 248 ff.; Arpee, *Awakening*, pp. 1–62.

[2] Arpee, *A History*, p. 239; Creasy, *op. cit.*, pp. 426 ff.; A. A. Adnan, "Turkey,
History," *Encyclopedia Brittannica*, ed. J. L. Garvin, Vol. XXII (1930).

[3] Der-Movsesian, *op. cit.*, II, 704, 729 ff.; Arpee, *A History*, pp. 248 ff.

[4] *Ibid.*; Lynch, *op. cit.*, II, 445 f.; Prime, *op. cit.*, pp. 480 ff.; Arpee, *Awakening*,
pp. 25 ff., 31 ff., 186 f.

ideas of reform and progress of the three Sultans.[1] Therefore, while Abdul Aziz was proclaiming security, freedom, and paternal care for all the subjects of his Empire—Muslim and Christian alike—his Grand Vizier, the *Shaikh-ul-Islam*, and the Minister of War plotted against him. The *Shaikh-ul-Islam* proclaimed a religious *Fetwa* (edict), announcing the deposition of Abdul Aziz as harmful to the interests of the Ottoman Empire and the Muslim religion. In five days the Sultan was found assassinated.

His son and successor, Murad V, being of the same mind, invited Zia Bey—the leader of the Young Turk Party—to head his government, but the *Ulama*, with similar fanaticism and earnest visions of Pan-Islamism, had him also dethroned by another religious *Fetwa*—denouncing him as a friend of the *infidels* and as mentally incapable.

Murad's rule ended within three months. His brother Abdul Hamid II, the "red Sultan of Turkey," succeeded him. The old school Turks found in Hamid a typically Turkish and able leader, full of cunning, cruelty, devilish intelligence, diplomatic versatility, and Islamic fanaticism. He wanted to rule as the supreme head of the Empire as well as of Islam. He thought of himself as "the shadow of God on earth."[2]

B. Turkey and Armenian Nationalism

The accession of Abdul Hamid II proved to be a plague for the Armenians as a nation. For, as soon as Hamid was on the throne, he set himself to liberate the Empire from foreign interferences and impositions. *One* of the major causes of the European intervention in Turkish domestic affairs was the question of *reforms* promised by his predecessors to the Christian minorities in general and the Armenians in particular.

The powers of Europe had just recently presented a note to this effect (May 12, 1876). They called a conference in Constantinople to discuss the reforms of conditions in the provinces of Turkey (December 11, 1876). On December 23 of the same year, Hamid and his Grand

---

[1] "Ulama," *A Dictionary of Islam*; "Shaikh al Islam," *Encyclopedia of Islam*, Vol. IV (1934); Der-Movsesian, *op. cit.*, II, 735 ff.; Creasy, *op. cit.*, pp. 528–549. *Ulama*, headed by the *Shaikh-ul-Islam*, formed "the theocratic element of the government in Muslim countries." The *Shaikh-ul-Islam*, a member of the Turkish Cabinet, was appointed by the Sultan.

[2] Der-Movsesian, *op. cit.*, II, 758 ff.; W. Miller, *The Ottoman Empire*, 1801–1913 (Cambridge: Cambridge University Press, 1913), pp. 46 ff., 147 ff., 298 ff., 364 ff.

Vizier Midhat proclaimed the Turkish Constitution, pretending to satisfy the demands of the European powers.[1]

The next year Russia declared war on Turkey (April 24, 1877); Turkey was defeated, and Constantinople was saved from Russian occupation only by the entrance of the British fleet into the Dardanelles (February 13, 1878). The Treaty of San Stefano settled the war between the two neighbors, giving Russia every right to supervise reforms in the Armenian provinces, and, if need be, to re-occupy that section of the Ottoman Empire. *England resented this.*[2]

Forthwith England demanded a European congress to reconsider the provisions of the Treaty of San Stefano. It met in Berlin on July 13, 1878, with six European powers present.[3] The provision of reforms in Armenia was recast into Article 61 of the Berlin Treaty, England being granted executive authority to supervise it. Cyprus was occupied as a gurantee. *These new provisions greatly displeased* the Russians. Mutual rivalries paralyzed the plan. Soon England had to withdraw its consuls of supervision because of Russian opposition and general European rivalries. Now neither Russia nor England was responsible for Armenian reforms. Hamid felt his hands free to perpetrate his fiendish schemes. And he did.[4]

Unfortunately, the Armenian "revolutionary" bands, organized in face of desperate conditions in the provinces, gave the much desired *pretext* for general massacres. These bands were organized to force the hands of the signatory powers of the Berlin Treaty, but they were badly mistaken.[5] Hamid was too astute and ruthless for that. He ordered the slaughter of the innocent population of the Armenian provinces, which constituted a pattern up to the year 1920. In half a century, the Armenians in Turkey were reduced from over two millions to about fifty thousand souls in 1920. Half of them were actually slain or lost to Islam, and the other half was expelled or migrated from Turkey.

It is commonplace to claim that the Turks massacred the Armenians because of their Christian faith. This is generally true. However, the Turks have also persecuted and imprisoned Muslim Arabs of Syria and Lebanon, and the Kurds in the 1920's, even though to a much less degree. Therefore, to point to religious fanaticism as the *sole* cause of the Armenian massacres does not satisfy our critical historical sense. When

---

[1] Arpee, *Awakening*, p. 35.

[2] Miller, *op. cit.*, pp. 384 ff., 387 ff., 395 ff.

[3] England, France, Russia, Germany, Italy, Austria-Hungary, with Turkey.

[4] Toynbee, *op. cit.*, pp. 617–626; Miller, *op. cit.*, pp. 427 ff.

[5] *Ibid.*; Arpee, *A History*, p. 296 ff.

religious persecutions *did* occur, they were *localized* looting and pillaging of churches, occasional coercion to apostasy, and some actual slaying of worshippers and clergymen. But when the fanaticism of Pan-Islamic dreams united with the policy of Ottomanisation of the nationalist Young Turk Party, then the plot was concocted to wipe out a subject people—the Armenians. For, they were not only of the enemy faith, but also were a hindrance to the Pan-Turanian dreams and aspirations by their geographical position, demand for local reforms, invitation to European intervention, and, ultimately, political autonomy and independence.[1]

Therefore, it must be stated again, that throughout their long history, the Armenian people were first facing a wild, cruel, Mongolian tribe in its Seljuk and Ottoman offshoots. Secondly, they faced an alien religion claiming absolute supremacy and final obedience, granting them the right to live on condition of the head tax—*jizyah*. Thirdly, and most basically, they were in polar opposition to the nationalistic dreams of the Young Turk Party which aimed at a Pan-Turanian, Pan-Islamic, Turkish Empire with which the Armenian national aspirations were irreconcilable.

There was only one solution: either the Armenians had to forego their legitimate rights of political equality, or they had to forfeit their right to live in a hostile Muslim state. The Armenians could not abandon their rights; but the Turks could quite conveniently impose the second. For, according to the Islamic Law, no subject race or country can enjoy the protection of a Muslim state unless it abides a loyal tributary.[2]

The Armenians in Turkey had been always a faithful people, serving the highest interests of the Ottoman Empire; but their legitimate national aspirations were interpreted and misinterpreted as disloyalty to the Turkish-Muslim state. And the Muslim faith would not hesitate fighting those who would not submit either to the faith or to its Caliph as tributary subjects. Therefore, the Turkish nationalists were never hesitant to order the extermination of a people who were considered the enemies of politico-nationalistic dreams of Pan-Turanian Ottomanisation and a thorn in the side of Pan-Islamic dreams.[3]

Unfortunately, this was not clearly grasped by the patriotic Armenian revolutionaries whose sole aim was to deliver the helpless population

---

[1] Toynbee, *op. cit.*, pp. 634 ff., 637 ff.; Miller, *op. cit.*, pp. 477–481.

[2] "Jizyah," "Zimmah," and "Zimmi," *A Dictionary of Islam*; *Quran*, 9:7–10.

[3] Toynbee, *op. cit.*, p. 634; Tabari, *op. cit.*, pp. 154 ff.; "*Covenant of Umar*", *op. cit.*

of the interior from the tyranny of the Turks and Kurds. They put too much trust in the goodwill and friendship of the so-called "Christian" "Great Powers" of Europe. The Armenians had forgotten that political and economic self-interest is always closer than the interest in the welfare of a distant neighbor.

The Catholicos of the Armenians, the Patriarchs of Constantinople and Jerusalem, the Catholicos of Cilicia, and the Armenian Church, should have given wise guidance to the Armenians, but they, too, had been *identified* with the national aspirations.

C. The Armenian Church and Nationalism

It has been reiterated heretofore that the Armenian Church was identified with the national aspirations of its people. Ever since the loss of Armenian political independence, the Catholici of the Armenian Church had discharged the dual duty of spiritual and temporal head of the nation. The *Ulama* and the Young Turks could not mistake this about the Armenian Church.

During the war of 1877–1878, Russia had posed as the protector of the Slavic Christians in the Turkish Empire. She intervened on behalf of them, securing independence for Rumania, Serbia, and Montenegro, by the Treaty of San Stefano (March 3, 1878).

During these negotiations, *Patriarch Nerses Varjabedian* of Constantinople appealed to Duke Nicholas for reforms in the Armenian provinces. Thereupon, the Duke had the provision inserted in Article XVI of the San Stefano Treaty that should Turkey refuse to undertake immediate reforms in Armenia, the Russian troops would return to occupy the Armenian provinces.[1]

Such a provision, as noted before, was not only displeasing to England, but aggravating to Hamid. Naturally, more to Hamid, because a subject race under his rule had appealed to his enemy for protection. It is not hard to perceive the political implications of such an undiplomatic move.

But the more so, because the appeal was made by one—the Armenian Patriarch of Constantinople—who ascended that throne and exercised its authority only as an official of the Turkish Government and by the pleasure, permission, and tolerance of the Sultan. He was appointed as the head of the Armenian Church, the administrative representative,

---

[1] Addison, *op. cit.*, pp. 59 ff.; Der-Movsesian, *op. cit.*, II, 759; Ormanian, *History*, III, cols. 4339–4349; Miller, *op. cit.*, pp. 382 ff.

and the leader of the religious and civil affairs of the Armenian "millet" in Turkey. Whereas, here he was entering the province of politics, and that not with or on behalf of the Sultan and his Empire, but appealing to the enemies of the Sultan for protection against him.

By the provision of the Treaty of San Stefano Russia was sure of achieving two political aims: first, recognizing well the fact that Hamid would be unwilling to prosecute the reform, it would permit the occupation of this fertile and strategic land of Armenian provinces; secondly, by occupying Armenia, Russia would have the door to India and the Far East wide open before her.

Both of these considerations were diametrically opposed to the imperialistic and colonial interests of Albion. Hence the demand of the Congress of Berlin incited by Great Britain.[1]

The second great blunder which the Armenian Patriarch appears to have made was during the Congress of Berlin (1878). Sultan Hamid cleverly persuaded the same Patriarch Varjabedian to present the claims of Armenian reforms at the Congress of Berlin also. Thereupon, the delegation of two bishops—Mgrdich Khrimian and Khoren Narbey— and two laymen, Minas Cheraz and Stepan Papazian, was appointed and sent to Berlin.[2] They were not received into the Conference room, but the Armenian claims were incorporated into Article 61 of the Berlin Treaty, often called "the death warrant of the Armenian nation." Wily Hamid was past master of power politics, adept in playing one power against another. Reforms never came. The Armenians were liquidated.

There is no need to go into the details of the mass meetings, agitations, speeches, and celebrations, where often the Armenian clergy presided. This writer can vividly remember the bearing and exhibition of arms by Armenian young people, specially the members of the revolutionary parties.

The Armenian clergy, instead of giving sound moral advice and political guidance, often acquiesced in these activities. As individuals all men owe the duty of earnest patriotism. But when those individuals represent a nation and their church but forget the counsel of wisdom for national aspirations, one wonders who should be blamed more: Abdul Hamid and his cohorts who had no moral or humane scruples toward a subject race; no fear of international intervention because of European

---

[1] Toynbee, *op. cit.*, pp. 622 ff.; Arpee, *A History*, pp. 295 ff.; F. D. Green, *Armenian Massacres, or The Sword of Mohammad* (Philadelphia: International Publishing Co., 1896), pp. 76–86.

[2] Der-Movsesian, *op. cit.*, II, 763–765; Ormanian, *History*, III, col. 4345.

mutual rivalries; no religious scruples, because of *Quranic* sanctions to fight the unbelievers; and had every physical and military means in hand to exterminate a helpless, unprotected, rural, and peaceful, Christian minority? Or, the hierarchy, leaders, and political extremists of the Armenian Church and nation, who were utterly naive to trust the goodwill and promises of the great powers; who appealed to the very enemies of the Sultan and Empire; who gave the pretext of revolt by organizing revolutionary bands; who demonstrated in front of the Summer Palace—*Yildiz*—of Hamid, and occupied the Banque Ottoman in Constantinople; who fought against the Turkish regulars without preparing the nation for self-defense; who underestimated the wile, cruelty, and shrewdness of Hamid and his court, and relied on the polished and diplomatic pledges of the fanatic and nationalistic Young Turks who ultimately schemed and executed the plan of the total extermination of Armenians in Turkey?

The judgment was inevitable. A small minority which had struggled against great odds to preserve its identity, faith, and culture, was finally on the highway to progress and gradual liberation—as noted above. Political ideologies of European revolutions—with slogans of liberty, equality, and fraternity—had thrilled the hearts of all subject peoples everywhere, including the Armenians.

However, zealot revolutionaries and nationalistic elements—devoid of all diplomatic sense and political experience and lacking the wisdom of sound statesmanship—appear to have exposed a host of helpless people to the merciless ravages of a cruel wolf, Abdul Hamid II and his court.

And in all of these tragic circumstances, the hierarchy and clergy of the Armenian Apostolic Church appear to have acquiesced or actively participated in the movements that resulted in destruction. The Armenian Church—as a Christian institution—could have stood on a humanitarian and moral plane and given sound leadership and advice to her people. Then it might have acted as the intermediary and intercessor for her nation. But, on the contrary, it seems to have identified itself with the national aspirations of the Armenians, and the outcome was ruin for the nation as well as the church.[1]

---

[1] Toynbee, *op. cit.*, pp. 637–653; Ormanian, *History*, III, cols. 4342 ff., 4366 ff., 4404 ff.; Arpee, *A History*, pp. 238 ff., 266 ff.; E. G. Mears, *Modern Turkey: A Politico-Economic Interpretation, 1908–1923* (New York: The Macmillan Company, 1924), pp. 63 ff., 66 ff.; Green, *op. cit.*, *passim*; Adnan, "Turkey, History," *Encyclopedia Britannica*, Vol. XXII (1930).

D. CHRISTOLOGY, NATIONALISM, AND POLITICS

The vicious circle was completed. To recapitulate: The Armenian Church, first alienated from the church in Caesarea on administrative and jurisdictional as well as national considerations, finally broke with the Church of the Empire on Christological grounds. Christology became instrumental in segregating the Armenian Christians and in preserving their Church as a national heritage. The Armenian Church, self-isolated by Christological position and nationalized to withstand Greek persecutions, encroachments, and assimilation, endeavored to preserve the nation intact. This it accomplished by conserving the Armenian language, literature, and traditions amidst alien peoples, cultures, and religions. The doctrinally isolated and ecclesiastically nationalized church identified itself with the aspirations of the Armenian nation and ventured into the field of aggressive politics. When these aspirations, however legitimate, encountered the Turkish nationalism, the Armenian Church, its people, and Armenian politico-revolutionary ideologies appeared to be inseparable, as they had now been united in aims and aspirations. And when the Muslim-Turkish nationalists decided to strike the final death blow, it did so indiscriminately to nationalist-revolutionary elements, the common people, and their national church, because they had become "one nation indivisible."

Obviously, the Christology which had preserved the Armenian Church as a distinctly national church and heritage had also become the source of its sufferings.[1] What it had helped to conserve—a national church—now faced destruction by the conflict of those nationalistic aspirations and dreams with the Muslim-Turkish nationalism.

Therefore, conversely, what the Church had so ardently advocated and faithfully preserved—namely, the Monophysite Christology and the consequent fervent nationalism—appears to have been the cause and source of its misfortunes.

We have already noted the involvement of the Armenian Patriarch in nationalistic affairs of the people, depriving him of the prestige and influence of a wise and religious shepherd.

It must be added further, that, as in the case of Armeno-Arab relations, so in Armeno-Turkish relations, the Monophysite Christology of the Armenian Church was a barrier to the building of an intellectual bridge between the two religious groups. For, while the progressive

---

[1] Ormanian, *History*, I, col. 514; Der-Nersessian, *op. cit.*, pp. 29 ff.; Kidd, *op. cit.*, p. 436.

Sultans were contemplating reforms, the religious caste of the *Ulama*, with their *Shaikh-ul-Islam*, was conspiring against their Sultans and their Christian subjects. Undoubtedly, the opposition of the religious caste was based on the Islamic law and Pan-Islamic dreams, as that of the Young Turks was based on the nationalism of Pan-Turanian dreams.[1] They were led even to suspect that Sultan Mahmud himself might be an infidel in pledging justice and mercy to the Christians. The Sultans were liquidated by religious edicts (*Fetwa*) and Abdul Hamid enthroned.

One need not be a scholar of Islam to discern that the fanatical antagonism of the religious caste of Turkey had as much share in Hamid's atrocities as the fanatic nationalism of the Young Turks. The Sultan as Caliph was the head of the entire Muslim world. The *Shaikh-ul-Islam* was the supreme judge of the Muslims in the Ottoman capital and Empire. Under his jurisdiction a group of Christians were living and agitating for reforms, and, ultimately, independence of the Muslim yoke. These Christians were worshippers of Jesus (*Isa*) as God and adoring his mother as "Mother of God."

This religious creed could have no contact with the faith of Islam and its intellectuals. Muslims had never conferred on Jesus the title of Son of God. This was blasphemy. Besides, Muhammad was the seal of prophets. He was superior to Jesus. Therefore, Christianity was the inferior religion.

When the religious caste of Turkey was plotting against the Armenians, they would seem to have the satisfaction of Saul of Tarsus, as doing service to *Allah* and true religion. In the destruction of Armenians they would have the gratification of destroying an idolatrous, polytheistic, infidel, and intransigent element—the blasphemers of God's name and rebels against Muslim rule. The Prophet had ordered them to fight those who gave a companion to God and called Jesus the son of God.

Unfortunately, the Armenian Christians, their Church, Liturgy, Christology, greatly contributed to this misconception. Their emphasis was so little on the human life of Jesus Christ and so much on "Christ our God." To be sure, the Liturgy spoke of the Incarnation, but we have discovered that this Incarnate Word dwelt in the flesh with divine qualities, attributes, and nature. This made the Incarnation superficial.[2]

---

[1] Tabari, *op. cit.*, p. 156, and note 4; Der-Movsesian, *op. cit.*, II, 715; *supra*, pp. 98 ff.

[2] G. Kruger, "Monophysitism," *Encyclopedia of Religion and Ethics*, ed. J. Hastings, Vol. VIII (1922); "Monophysites," *Encyclopedia Britannica*, Vol. XV, 14th ed.

Manifestly, all of these would look like anthropolatry to the Muslim mind. It could appear to Islam nothing else but that the Armenian Monophysites were worshipping the form of human life as "Christ our God." This was anathema, blasphemy, and sacrilege for Islam.[1] Therefore, the plot to exterminate the Armenians had four basic motives behind it: (1) to get rid of an element which had become a cause of European intervention in Turkish domestic affairs; (2) to liquidate a minority race which insisted on its national identity and ultimate independence, irreconcilable with Turkish nationalism and Ottomanization; (3) to do away with a group of Christians who were worshipping the prophet Jesus as God, the greatest sin for the Muslims; (4) and to destroy an institution—the Armenian Church—which was playing treasonable politics with the great powers of Europe.

Thus, the Church of Armenians—founded and preserved at the cost of the blood and sacrifice of many martyrs—instead of becoming a missionary institution and an active light among the Muslims, had become the enemy of the ruling political caste as it was of the religious caste.

Consequently, it so appears that the divine verdict was pronounced: "Mene, mene, tekel upharsin."[2] By insisting on its Monophysite Christology, the Armenian Church had isolated itself from the world church. By self-isolation, it had become a national, self-contained, and defensive church. By identifying itself with the national aspirations of the race, it had ventured into the field of politics where it had encountered the ultranationalism of Turkish Pan-Turanianism. And in religion, by Christ-worship it confronted the fanaticism of the ultra-mono-theistic *Ulamas* and *Mullas*.[3]

And when the opportune moments arrived—in 1876, 1895, 1909, 1915–1918, and 1920—ALL of these antagonists joined hands to exterminate a people, a church, a religious stand, a political aspiration, which, however legitimate and humanly natural, had become inimical, offensive, and obnoxious to the interests of the Ottoman Empire as much as to Islam as the ruling and rival religion.

Thus, it again appears that the Monophysite Christology of the Armenian Church, by *creating* and *preserving* the Church of Armenia as a conspicuously non-conformist, unorthodox, and national institution,

---

[1] *Quran*, 9:30; 5:116, 117; 43:57–65; "Jesus Christ," *A Dictionary of Islam*.
[2] Daniel 5:25.
[3] "Mulla," *A Dictionary of Islam*; defined as "a learned man, a scholar, filled with knowledge."

had become the source of strength as well as weakness to the Armenian Church and its people. What it had helped to create and preserve had tresspassed the boundaries of Christian vocation and entered the realm of aggressive nationalism and politics.[1] These, in turn, combined with *Monophysitic isolation*,[2] obstructed the evangelization of the Muslim environment and served as factors contributing to the tragedies of the Armenian people and their martyred church.[3]

---

[1] e.g. By appealing to Duke Nicholas and sending delegates to the Berlin Congress. Cf. *supra*, pp. 102, 103.

[2] And other factors treated above; *passim*.

[3] Cf. *infra*, Appendix, Diagrams A-K, specially K; also, *supra*, pp. 15 ff., 36 ff., 63 ff., 87 ff.

PART FIVE

A RE-ORIENTATION OF THE ARMENIAN CHURCH

CHAPTER SEVEN

STEPS FOR DOCTRINAL, NATIONAL, AND ECCLESIASTICAL RE-ORIENTATION

If the analysis of the foregoing pages is correct and the conclusions reached are valid, they imply that the Armenian Church and its people need a re-orientation in their doctrinal, ecclesiastical, and national position. This necessitates some radical steps to be taken. It will require some serious revisions of past attitudes, relations, and policies.

We will venture to make some suggestions as to the next steps to remedy the failures and misunderstandings of the past.

A. Revision of the Armenian Christology

Heretofore, this dissertation has tried to point out the Monophysite Christology of the Armenian Church as one of the major causes of its isolation, nationalization, and the resultant historical tragedies of the Armenian people. Therefore, in an effort to remedy the past and to adopt a new orientation, the first step to be taken is the reconsideration and revision of the Armenian Christology. This need not be the compromise of *truth*, but an effort better to understand and represent the doctrine of the Incarnation and its implications.

The doctrine of the Incarnation and its corollary, Christology, are the perennial subjects of discussion for Christian thinkers. If the Armenian Church is to occupy its rightful position within the family of the Christian churches everywhere, certain elemental factors must be recognized and clarified.

The historical Monophysite doctrine was a definition motivated by a desire to preserve the divine element in the redemption through Christ. For this we should appreciate the efforts and sincerity of the Armenian and other Monophysites. However, it must also be recognized that—as developed in the foregoing pages—the Cyrillian position was one-sided, that it weakened the force of the Incarnation,

> leaving out of account every element of human personality in the Savior... In principle, the *Logos* becomes flesh; in reality, however, the flesh becomes transformed into divine nature.[1]

---

[1] Kruger, "Monophysitism," *Encyclopedia of Religion and Ethics*, Vol. VIII (1922); H. Hausheer, "Monophysitism," *An Encyclopedia of Religion*, ed. V. Ferm, one volume, 1945.

Thus, by insisting on the one-nature formula of Cyril, the Mono-physite position tampered with the humanity of the Incarnate Word, and thereby the orthodox, patristic, *Logos* soteriology was practically denied. For, patristic soteriology was rooted in the conviction that man was to be *deified* and saved by union with the Son of God just as the divine nature was *humanized* in the act of the Incarnation. "He was made what we are that He might make us what He is Himself," had declared Irenaeus.[1] According to the one-nature formula, this was not true; and, if so, it meant that the divine nature was not truly human-ized; there is no real affinity between the divine and human natures; and, consequently, human nature cannot be redeemed and deified through salvation.

Although Gregory of Datev had written that "we confess the death and passion of God become man,"[2] still it was not the Word *truly become flesh*, but "the Word becoming flesh and *uniting our nature perfectly with his Deity*."[3]

The word "with" is very significant. The Incarnate Word is said to be *united with* human nature and flesh, but not actually become human. This was the absorption of the humanity in the divinity of the Incarnate Word.[4]

Therefore, it seems to be imperative for the Armenian Church to correct this position of holding the doctrine of a partial Incarnation. We recognize that in the year of grace 1965 we cannot endorse fully all that Chalcedon did. We can find flaws in its mysterious, and seeming-ly contradictory, definition of the person of Christ. And yet, it achieved one goal which should be admitted and preserved—namely, the full revelation of God in a fully and completely human personality was unequivocally re-affirmed. By officially accepting this definition, the Armenian Church can remove the stigma of "heresy" from the fore-head of a faithful Christian church and people.

To accomplish this end, the Armenian Church can approach the Christological problem from the modern view of man and personality, and in its creedal reconversion it can present a modern definition of the Incarnation—while remaining faithful to the Gospel truth and the historical fact.

---

[1] Walker, *op. cit.*, p. 66*; Baillie, *op. cit.*, p. 129.
[2] Arpee, *A History*, p. 182.
[3] *Ibid.*, p. 181, underscoring is mine; *supra*, pp. 47 ff.
[4] Cf. *supra*, pp. 43 ff.; 53 ff.

* *Used by permission.*

For, obviously, the Chalcedonian creed has been severely criticised by ancient as well as modern liberal theology. The two-nature formula implied that only the human nature born of Mary was crucified and suffered, thus reverting to the Platonic view of the impassibility of the Deity—which the school of Antioch approved while the Alexandrians tried to avoid. Therefore, the first of these schools insisted on the distinction of the two natures; the latter stressed the unity of the two. Hence the rejection of the phrase of Peter the Fuller of Antioch—"who was crucified for us," "the symbol of the Monophyistes," which the Chalcedonian orthodoxy denounced.[1]

The Armenian and other Monophysites, rightly, strove to preserve the conviction that God suffered on the cross; that the divine heart and His love were betrayed there, And yet, it was the divine actually revealed in and through the real, complete, and full humanity of Jesus Christ.

The Armenian Church, therefore, can officially point to the inadequacy of the classical terms of nature, substance, hypostasis, and person, and advocate the necessity of interpreting the person of Christ in terms of the unity of spiritual personality. For God is Spirit, and spirit is free, creative, and self-conscious. Man also is a free self and subject, with a *spirit* derived from God. The self-conscious and creative spirit of man is dependent on God for its completion and perfection. The more man lives in dependence on God, the more he becomes identified with God.

Jesus of Nazareth, a man with human spirit and a free subject, had perfectly identified his creative freedom, will, and mind, with God's Spirit, holy will, self-sacrificing love, and creativity, considering himself to be one with the Father—as the Fourth Gospel reports it. Thus, he had become the perfect man, realizing the full aim of human personality by living in complete dependence on God and in perfect obedience to Him.[2]

And yet, he was "perfectly divine as to his Godhead"—as the creeds put it—in that God as Spirit and free Subject fully dwelt in him, and loved, worked, suffered, and saved the world, through him. Thus, the Chalcedonian formula is preserved, that is, perfect God and perfect

---

[1] Adeney, *op. cit.*, pp. 113–114*; Baillie, *op. cit.*, pp. 151 ff.; J. S. Lawton, *Conflict in Christology* (London: Society for Promoting Christian Knowledge, 1947), pp. 26 ff., *passim*.

[2] John 14:8 ff.; 4:34 ff.; 6:38 ff.

* *Used by permission.*

man as spiritual subjects are united in one person of Jesus Christ. This would also overcome the mistake of Chalcedon, ascribing impassibility to the divine nature; and the Monophysite error, minimizing and almost ignoring the truly human person of the Incarnate Word.

By this revision, it could be said that the passion of Christ was the passion of God; that God "was crucified for us"; but only vicariously in and through Jesus of Nazareth, rather than God physically hanging on the cross.

As many moderns have attempted to reinterpret the Chalcedonian definition, the Armenian Church should not hesitate to reconsider its own position and declare its adherence to the symbol of Chalcedon. In the past, many of its Catholici have consented to accept and adopt it—as seen on the foregoing pages—the most famous of them being Nerses the Graceful of Cilicia (ca. 1166–1173).[1] But, suspicions of Nestorian teaching, jurisdictional rivalry, and the fears of national assimilation obstructed the reunion of the Armenian Church with the Church of the Empire. Now, it is possible for the Catholicos to call a synod of bishops and laymen, formally to adopt the orthodox creed and to undertake its reinterpretation and re-formulation.

However, the approach to Chalcedon and Christology should be based on the spiritual concept of personality. The major question in Christology is the relation of divinity to humanity in Christ. As stated before, the essence of personality is spiritual—the self-conscious, free, self-determining, and creative, spirit of man.[2] Jesus of Nazareth, by living in constant dependence on God and obedience to His will, was the perfect person and personality. Through the perfect communion and self-identification with God's will the Divine Spirit dwelt in him fully. Thereby, in him dwelt the fullness of the Godhead. He was perfectly human, yet perfectly divine, in spirit. Both God's Spirit and the spirit of Jesus were the subject of the life of the Son of Man.

Such an approach might avoid the Apollinarian error of ascribing to Christ an "impersonal humanity"; the Cyrillian error of the absorption of the human by the divine in Christ; and the Chalcedonian error of dualism of nature in one person, while preserving the truth that God's perfect revelation came in perfect humanity. It would avoid

---

[1] *Supra*, pp. 17 ff.; T. Poladian, "An Armenian Reply to the Pope," *The Christian Century*, LVIII (December, 1951), pp. 1513–1514.

[2] W. D. Mackenzie, "Jesus Christ," *Encyclopedia of Religion and Ethics*, Vol. VII (1922); J. E. McTaggart, "Personality," *Encyclopedia of Religion and Ethics*, Vol. IX (1924).

further the error of modern Kenotic theory of a depotentiated God.[1]

The Armenian Church should not delay any further to re-examine its doctrinal position in the light of modern psychology and theology, return to the fold of orthodox Christianity, and initiate a new definition of the person of Christ.

However, the Armenian Church must solve the problem of its relationship to the nation and its aspirations along with its doctrinal position, as they have been long identified and have supported one another. This leads us to the next step.

B. RECOGNITION OF THE SUPRA-NATIONAL CHARACTER OF THE CHURCH

The idea of nationality seems to be a historical heritage of all peoples everywhere, however late it may have emerged. St. Paul spoke of all nations "made of one blood... (and) the bounds of their habitation."[2]

These boundaries of nationality have been designated by modern writers as "race, language, culture, religion, and geography."[3] Nationality has been variously defined: as a subjective sentiment produced by many factors, such as race, language, geography, religion, culture, history, tradition, and common economic interests;[4] a state of mind;[5] as the self-consciousness of a nation;[6] as a spiritual possession, a way of feeling, thinking, and living.[7]

According to these definitions, the Armenians constitute a nation and have the right to be attached to their nationality.[8] For, they claim a distinct origin, language, country, religion, art, literature, architecture, music, and a history—at times glorious, at others tragic.

---

[1] Baillie, *op. cit.*, pp. 79–97; Lawton, *op. cit.*, pp. 23–43; W. Sanday, *Christology and Personality*, I. *Christologies Ancient and Modern*: II. *Personality in Christ and in Ourselves* (New York: Oxford University Press, American Branch, 1911), I:1–56; II:1–75.

[2] Acts, 17:24–26.

[3] Marquess of Lothian *et. al. The Universal Church and the World of Nations*, Vol. VII of *The Official Oxford Conference Books* ("World Conference on Church, Community, and State"; Chicago: Willett, Clark, and Co., 1938), p. 4 f.

[4] K. Page, *Imperialism and Nationalism* (New York: George H. Doran Co., 1925), p. 23.

[5] *Ibid.*, p. 23, citing L. Zangwill, *The Principle of Nationalities* (London: Watts, 1917).

[6] Page, *op. cit.*, p. 23, citing G. P. Gooch, *Nationalism* ("Swarthmore International Handbooks"; New York; Harcourt, Brace & Co., Inc., 1920).

[7] Page, *op. cit.*, citing Alfred D. Zimmern without giving the title of the source; p. 23.

[8] S. Bryant, "Nationality," *Encyclopedia of Religion and Ethics*, Vol. IX (1924); Der-Nersessian, *op. cit., passim.*

Therefore, we cannot condemn the Armenian people for loving their nation much. Which nation has not loved its own nationality, even to the point of nationalistic imperialism and aggression? But, in the realm of Christian revelation and Church the picture is altogether different. Here nation and nationality are transcended by ideals which are supra-national, supra-racial, and supra-mundane.

The Christological secession of the Armenian Church firmly established and perpetuated the ecclesiastical autonomy initiated by King Bab (ca. 371). Once the Empire Church stigmatized them as "heretical" and the Armenians persistently refused to recognize Chalcedon, the religious isolation of the Armenian Church was determined once for all. Now, Church and State found mutual allies for mutual defense. At times they were at odds, but ordinarily the Crown and the Pontiff of the Armenian Church were allies in fighting for the religious and political independence of the nation. And, finally, when the political throne of Armenia was abolished, the head of the Church was allowed to perform not only his religious functions, but also the civil function of administering the affairs of the nation under the "millet" system of the Ottoman Empire.[1]

Presently, and almost inevitably, what began as the administration of religious and civil affairs of a subject people ended with the function of protecting the national, cultural, and *political* rights of the Armenian minority. The outcome is writ large in history. It is granted that the Armenian Church and its head had every right to serve the civilian interests of the Armenians, but when the realm of politics was tresspassed, the judgment was inescapable. The Church was oblivious of the fact that it had a supra-national origin and goal, was an inter-racial fellowship, and had a spiritual function—namely, to build a kingdom where Jew and Gentile, Armenian and Turk, Arab and Persian, were called to unite.[2]

Unfortunately, the Armenian Church, having identified itself with the nation, could no more witness to the supra-national Gospel of Christ—the power of God unto salvation, *even of the oppressing enemies.* We have examined the fact that the Monophysite Christology had no intellectual appeal to the Muslim theologian and layman. Now, the nationalistic garb of the Church would make absolutely no appeal to the nationalistic Turks, or Arabs. It could not invite them to a fellowship where the distinction of color, race, or nationality disappears,

---

[1] Toynbee, *op. cit.*, pp. 617 ff.
[2] Lothian, *op. cit.*, p. 20.

because the Church itself had become exclusively the Church of the Armenians. It had been transformed into an institution concerned more with the ecclesio-doctrinal identity of the Church and the politico-national rights of its people than the obligations of evangelizing its environment.

The fact of Muhammadan prevention of preaching and proselytization is quite beside the point. The Church had already lost its missionary zeal by Christological disputes and defensive isolationism. When the Muslim state ruled over it, no evangelistic vitality had survived to proclaim the Gospel to the Muslims, because the Church itself had been embroiled in the political and national aspirations and upheavals of its own people. So much so, that even to our day, the Armenian Church is made into an arena of political party feuds. Unscrupulous zealots have always attempted to use the Church as an instrument of their political ideologies and activities.[1]

One feels humiliated to record the assassination of an unprotected Archbishop—Leontius Tourian of New York—while officiating at the celebration of the Christmas Mass on Christmas Eve, 1933, in the Armenian Church of New York.[2] This crime was not committed for religious edification and doctrinal purity!!! The victim was a *clergyman*, the ruling Bishop of the Armenians in the United States, with pro-Soviet sympathies, while the murderers were said to belong to the anti-Soviet party expelled from Armenia in 1920. The Armenian Church was reaping the fruits of nationalistic zeal with which it had identified itself.

Therefore, it is evident that to recover its religious vitality and evangelistic zeal the Armenian Church should rectify its position and attitude towards nationalism. While serving the Armenians, it should recognize the fact of its belonging to a supra-national order of creation, and endeavor to be a Christian Church for *all* with whom it comes into contact.

The problem of language is quite irrelevant, because there were many Turks and Kurds in the Armenian provinces who spoke and understood Armenian; and there existed many churches, as in the province of Cilicia, where the use of Turkish was imposed upon the Armenians.

---

[1] Arpee, *A History*, pp. 244 ff., 248 ff.

[2] Arpee, *A History*, p. 308; cf. also *AZKATAV YEGHERNE* (The Crime of Betrayal of the Nation, New York: Gotchnag Press, 1935); *passim*. Series of Tourian Commission, No. 5.

It is superfluous to stress any further the implications and importance of the separation of the Armenian Church from nationalism. It parallels, in a minor degree, the Church-State issue in the American churches.[1]

If the Armenian Church would choose to rise above its Mono-physitic-nationalistic plane, it might be able to devote itself to the task of the evangelization of its Muslim environment in its present contacts in the Near Eastern countries. To do so, the Church should recognize that it is the only institution which speaks in the name of the living God, and with a prophetic judgment, to its own people as well as to the world. But when *any* church is totally identified with its nation, the prophetic voice would die and it would become subservient to political ideologies, parties, rulers, and states.

The sooner, therefore, the Armenian Church can revise its Mono-physitic-nationalistic mentality and policies, the quicker might its missionary spirit and zeal be revived. It is high time for the Armenian Church and its hierarchy to acknowledge the imperative nature of this re-orientation. It must realize that the Christian Church is "committed through faith in Christ to a new outlook on life and a new way of living."[2] Through its worship, preaching, witness, and action as an organized society, it should endeavor to possess the minds of its lay people and determine their conduct in daily private life.[3] Through the clergy—and, specially, the laity—it should strive to proclaim the Kingdom of God where race, color, and nationality are superseded by the *supra-national brotherhood of men* based on the consciousness of the *universal Fatherhood of God*.[4]

C. Co-operation with the World Church

One of the serious consequences of the Monophysite secession of the Armenian Church was the severance of its relations with the Eastern Orthodox (Greek) Church, which was creating a Christian Slavic civilisation, and with the Roman Church, which was building a Christian Europe.

To avoid national assimilation, it refused to return to the pale of the

---

[1] P. Blanshard, *American Freedom and Catholic Power* (Boston: The Beacon Press, 1951), pp. 295 ff., *passim*.

[2] W. A. Visser 't Hooft and J. J. Oldham, *The Church and Its Function in Society* (Chicago: Willett, Clark & Co., 1937), p. 176, *passim*.

[3] *Ibid.*, p. 177.

[4] K. S. Latourette *et al. Church and Community*, Vol. V of *The Official Oxford Conference Books* ("World Conference on Church, Community, and State"; Chicago: Willett, Clark & Co., 1938), pp. 97–105; 63–116.

Church Universal and has remained a schismatic institution, nor has it joined it later.[1] Beginning with the rupture in the sixth century, self-isolation seems to have been found more advantageous to the preservation of the ecclesiastical independence as well as national identity of Armenians. Hence, the historical opposition to the efforts to unite and cooperate with Christendom at large.

With equal claims to apostolicity, the Armenian Church has endeavored to remain and be recognized as a catholic and independent church—though the Roman Catholic Church rejects the claim of Armenian apostolicity. It has, therefore, refused to submit to Byzantium or Rome. And when political storms engulfed the Church and people of Armenia, the Eastern Orthodox churches—Greek, Russian, and others—were not concerned because of the "schismatic" position of Armenians; and the Roman Church denied assistance because of the religious "errors" of the Armenian Church.

It is evident that the Church of Armenia should make a serious effort to return to the fellowship of the World Church[2] by accepting the Chalcedonian symbol, recognizing its supra-national nature and calling, and perceiving its Christian obligation of loyalty to the Church Universal. *Doctrine* is important, but it should not be allowed to constitute a wall of separation. *Nationality* is precious, but as churches we aim at the supra-national kingdom of love and righteousness. *Ecclesiastical independence* is valuable, but as Christians and churches we are members of one another, obligated to seek the general health and welfare of the Body of Christ—the Church Universal.

If the menaces of secularism, communism, paganism, and Islam, are to be faced, no single church or communion can do it alone. The vision of the Kingdom of God should constrain all churches to sincere effort to unite and co-operate with the Church of the living God everywhere.[3]

As for its relations with the non-Protestant churches, better understanding could be secured by revising the Armenian Monophysite position and by rising above national preoccupations to world obligations. As has been maintained heretofore, Christology and nationalism have been close allies in preserving the independence of the Armenian Church and the identity of the Armenian people. Now the

---

[1] See *Supra*, Preface. We are gratified to record that in 1962 the two Sees of the Armenian Church—in Etchmiadzin (Soviet Armenia) and in Antilyas (near Beirut, Lebanon)—joined the World Council of Churches.

[2] Cf. *Supra*, Preface.

[3] *Ibid.*

Church of Armenia must retrace its steps to return to the orthodoxy of the Church Universal.

D. Revival of the Missionary Zeal

It is unfortunate that the dogmatic-schismatic-nationalistic position of the Armenian Church extinguished its missionary spirit.

It is a well known fact that the Christological disputes of the early centuries resulted in the petrifaction of the Eastern Churches. Dogma, dignity, ceremony, and rigid liturgy, were emphasized by all, forgetting their basic missionary calling. When ceremony and creedal formulae occupy the major attention of any church, the result is stultification and fossilization. The Armenian Church was not an exception.[1]

The Christological stand supported by the sacramental-liturgical status transformed the Armenian Church to a mystical institution wherein the believers sought comfort and safety, but neglected the task of evangelism.

The assaults of the Byzantine Empire and its Church had a large share in this situation, but it was only secondary. The basic internal indifference had already set in; the environmental factors further accentuated and confirmed the neglect of the missionary task. Beginning with the middle of the seventh century, the Persian and Muslim-Arab worlds were no more a missionary concern for the Armenian Church. Despite the *generally* tolerant attitude of the Muslim Caliphs, the Armenian and other Eastern Christians manifested no zeal and love to evangelize the Arab Muslims with the Gospel of Christ.

Reference has been made to L. Arpee's view that Muslim faith was more appealing to Arabs, Turks, and others than the moral discipline of the Christian faith.[2] It was answered that Turks and Tartars in Asia had embraced Christianity before embracing Islam.[3]

The fact of the matter is that when Islam confronted the Armenian Church and the other Christian communions of the Near East, they had *already* lost their message of a living Christ. Christ was "fossilized" under creedal formulae and worshipped as God through icons and images. Therefore, the Armenian Church—along with others—had no vital message to proclaim. Its prophetic voice was silent. The institution subsisted on doctrinal, ceremonialistic, and nationalistic diet.

---

[1] Adeney, *op. cit.*, p. 165; Walker, *op. cit.*, p. 159.
[2] Arpee, *A History*, pp. 201–203.
[3] Mingana, *op. cit.*, *passim*; Browne, *op. cit.*, pp. 9 f., 102 f.

Consequently, the pagan Arabs and Turks passed it by and turned to Islam.

During the thirteen centuries of the Muslim era, many Armenian synods are reported, many canons established, and many pronouncements made for reunion with the Greek Church, but we meet no significant official statement or effort to organize for missionary activity as in the days of St. Gregory and St. Mesrop. No thought was given to the translation of the Scriptures for the Arab world[1] as the forefathers had done for the Albanians and Georgians only two centuries earlier.

If it be said that the Christian churches were not awakened as yet to their missionary obligations, the command of the Lord—"Go ye to all nations"[2]—and the examples of the Armenian forefathers were there to instruct them.[3]

The truth seems to be that the Armenian Church—for reasons elucidated above—had lost its first love and missionary zeal for the neighboring peoples *because* it was concerned with the safeguarding of its own doctrinal position, ecclesiastical autonomy, and national integrity, rather than evangelistic activity.

It is imperative, therefore, that the Armenian Church should recover its former missionary spirit; revise its Monophysitic Christology, which does not possess a sufficiently strong appeal to Islam; return to the credal fold of the Church Universal and cooperate with it in the world wide efforts of evangelism;[4] rise to a supra-national consciousness, and rediscover its own particular missionary task—namely, the evangelization of the Muslim Near East.

Through this step by step regression, the Church of Armenia might recover and recapture the essence of the calling of the church—which is NOT doctrinal isolationism, or dogmatic ceremonialism, or exclusive concern with national culture and aspirations.[5] The supreme calling of the Christian Church—and of the Armenian Church—is to be a living, burning, aggressive, witness to a living Savior in the wilderness of secular and anti-Christian forces.

In this manner the Armenian Church can be the salt, savoring its

---

[1] The shining *exception* being the Persian and Arabic parellel translation of the New Testament by John of Julfa (Persia), who died in 1715 A.D. Cf. Arpee, *A History*, pp. 235 ff., 250 f.; Ormanian, *National History*, II, col. 2510 f.

[2] Matthew, 28:19 ff.

[3] Browne, *op. cit.*, p. 63; Mingana, *op. cit.*, *passim*; *supra*, p. 5.

[4] Cf. *Supra*, Preface, and note 1, p. 119.

[5] Der-Nersessian, *op. cit.*, pp. 29 ff.

environment; light, illuminating the surrounding darkness; a grain of wheat, to die and increase. This might occasion martyrdom again, yet not *only* to preserve one's own faith, doctrine, culture, and nationality, but martyrdom in the cause of the evangelization of the Muslim world and the pagan neighbors.

Such a door of opportunity was wide open for many centuries, but the Armenian Church could not enter it.

E. A New Armenian Approach to Muslims

If the Armenian Church will recover its missionary zeal for Islam, it must adopt some new methods of approach. For, even though almost totally expelled from Asia Minor, the Armenians are still a large colony of approximately 200,000[1] in the countries adjacent to Turkey. Due to the unfortunate experiences of the past six centuries, the Armenians have identified the Turks with Islam and Muslims in general. In popular psychology, if one is a Muslim—whether Arab, Persian, Egyptian, or Palestinian—he is called "Dajik", which is meant to be a synonym for Turk. This has created some unhappy reactions among the non-Turkish peoples of the Near East.

Therefore, the *first* step towards the evangelization of the Muslim environment is to distinguish the Turks from Islam; one being a *racial* group is limited to Turkey; the other is a *universal faith* with adherents all over the globe.

Second, the Armenian Church should make a serious effort to inform its constituency of the real nature of the Armeno-Muslim relations, emphasizing the fact that the Muslims *have not always massacred* the Armenians because of their Christian faith. On the contrary, many Caliphs have been rather tolerant toward Christian and the Armenian minorities.[2]

Third, the Armenian people should be informed of the fact that *in general* Islam and the *Quran* were friendly to the Christians as "the people of the Book," even though later Muhammad changed his attitude because of failure to win the Christians and the Jews to his creed. Therefore, the Armenians—and other Christians—can capitalize on the respect of Islam and *their* Book for Jesus as one of God's six prophets and on the friendly passages favoring them.[3]

---

[1] Latest estimates go as high as 500,000.
[2] Cf. *supra*, chapter V, pp. 70 ff.; Guillaume, *op. cit.*, pp. 132, 133.
[3] *Quran*, 3:40; 4:169; 15:29; 19:31; 43:59.

Fourth, Armenian and Muslim study circles should be organized to undertake a fair, open-minded, and friendly examination of the lives of Muhammad and Jesus; and the doctrines, traditions, and history of the two faiths should be zealously studied and compared by select mixed groups and the findings published in different languages of the countries concerned.

Fifth, the religion of Islam and the *Quran* should be studied as part of the curriculum of colleges and the higher grades of the secondary schools.

Sixth, an honest attempt should be made to get to the roots of the Muslim-Christian animosities, which are not altogether irreparable, as they are usually due to the misrule of *some* Caliphs on the Muslim side and to the resentments of the Crusades on the Christian side.[1]

Seventh, the Armenian Church should begin its denationalizing process and open its doors to *all* who may worship as Christian in its sanctuaries, irrespective of race, nationality, and cultural background. Although the Soviet regime may have partially imposed this process by depriving the churches and the Armenian Church of their civil and political functions; yet, the emphasis in Soviet Armenia still is on the *national* culture. Furthermore, the future of the church in Soviet Russia is altogether precarious because of the fact that the new generation is growing in an atheistic and materialistic atmosphere where the churches are again struggling for their own existence. Whereas, the Armenian Church in Syria, Lebanon, and elsewhere in the Near East, is free to amend its ultra-nationalistic stand and open its doors to all desiring to join it, without regard for racial background.

Eighth, a church that can rise to supra-national consciousness can, and should, preach true forgiveness of the enemies who persecuted and massacred its people. This is the true calling of the Church of Christ, of which the Armenian Church is a part and member. If the spirit of forgiveness can be cultivated, the relations of the two elements— Armenians and Muslims—could be harmonized and the peace of the Near East strengthened.

Lastly, the Muslim world should be offered a divine Savior who was genuinely human. So long as the Armenians and other Christians *insist* on the Trinitarian approach, the Muslim response will remain quite

---

[1] Browne, *op. cit.*, pp. 146, 135–145; Runciman, S., *A History of the Crusades*, Vol. I (Cambridge: At the University Press, 1951), *passim*; T. A. Archer and C. L. Kingsford, *The Crusades, The Story of the Latin Kingdom of Jerusalem* (5th impression; London: T. Fisher Unwin Ltd., 1919), *passim*.

negligible. The *starting point* should be the human life and perfect character of Jesus Christ whom Islam respects as *Isa-el-Masih* (Jesus the Messiah). The transition to the ever living Christ, the Son of God, should be made through moral teachings and spiritual principles[1] rather than doctrinal assertions—be they Monophysitic or Dyophysitic. Theological and Christological implications of the Christian Gospel should be considered in due course in an atmosphere of mutual friendship and confidence.[2]

In the final analysis, therefore, the new Armenian approach to Islam should start with the point where the Church severed itself from the Church of the majority. It should re-examine its interpretation of the Incarnation, proclaiming a divine yet perfectly human Christ; disengage itself from nationalistic and political entanglements and be the Church with a prophetic voice and a redeeming Gospel message; preach Christian forgiveness; devise ways and means of friendly contacts with Muslims, discuss Muslim-Christian relations and religious issues; and, finally, reconsider its missionary calling and devote itself to the task of the evangelization of its Muslim environment. If, in this manner, the Armenian Church can attain a non-sectarian and supranational consciousness, it might be willing to be martyred again. This time, however, not for doctrinal, ecclesiastical, and national identity *only*, but for the sake of the teeming millions of the Muslim Near East, so that the blood of her martyrs might become the seed of a Christian church won from the children of Ishmael.[3]

---

[1] Such as the Sermon on the Mount, the Two Great Commandments, The Golden Rule, Love, Service, and other Christian graces exemplified by Him (1 Cor. 13, Rom. 12).

[2] J. L. Barton, *The Christian Approach to Islam* (Boston: The Pilgrim Press, 1918), pp. 267–280.

[3] In this new Armenian approach to Muslims, I have not included the traditional means and methods of the missions in Muslim lands—such as hospitals, schools, literature, distribution of the Bible, and so forth. These are common knowledge now, being used and observed in every land where there are modern missions.

For further study of new methods of approach to Islam in the Near East, see *The International Review of Missions*, eds. N. Goodall and M. Sinclair, Vols. XXXV (1946), pp. 25–32; XXXVI (1947), 34–40; XXXVII (1948), 16–18; XXXVIII (1949), 32–40; XXXIX (1950), 32–40.

CHAPTER EIGHT

THE NEXT STEPS FOR ARMENIAN PROTESTANT CHURCHES

The first chapter of this essay was concluded with a brief summary of the birth and growth of the Armenian Evangelical Movement, which was due to the historical and religious causes surveyed on the foregoing pages. It was stated that the Armenian Apostolic Church had lost its spiritual vitality.

But the traditionally religious heart of the people was hungry for deeper experiences which they found in the evangelical—that is, Protestant—interpretation of salvation or justification by faith. And those who discovered this truth staked everything to keep and propagate it. The outcome was the break with the national church—often called "the mother Church"—and the organization of the first Armenian Evangelical Church in Constantinople on July 1, 1846, officially named "The Evangelical Church of Armenia."

Even though we deplore the imposed separation of the Evangelicals, yet it has been a blessing in disguise for the Armenian Apostolic Church as well as for the dissenters. It is beyond the scope of this thesis to review the lasting contributions of the Armenian Protestant Church during its century-long history. The religious, educational, and social life of the Armenian nation has been leavened by the influence of this spiritual movement.

And yet, with all its highly commendable contributions, the Armenian Evangelical Church was unable to capture the vision of the basic calling of the Christian Church—namely, the evangelization of Islam. To be sure, spasmodic efforts were made by individuals and personal contacts attempted, but no general fervor for missionary approach to Islam stirred the Armenian Protestant community. After a period of sixty to seventy-five years of Protestantism among Armenians (1846–1921), this writer, for instance, recalls *no* sermons preached by his pastors in the churches of Tarsus and Alexandria, stressing the task and duty of evangelization of the Muslim environment. Nor, therefore, was the Armenian Apostolic Church awakened to the responsibility of missionary service among Muslims as it had adopted some of the other constructive aspects of Evangelical Christianity. It is hard to tell whether this end would have been attained had the doors remained open.

The fact remains that the rise of the Armenian Protestant Church did not solve the basic problem faced in this dissertation. The zeal of evangelization of Islam did not thrill the hearts of the Protestant Armenians. These reformed churches also failed in their calling to be the missionaries and witnesses to Muslims. The imposition of *death penalty* on converts from Islam has been already faced and answered in our introduction. Furthermore, some relaxation of this law had been secured through the official intervention of the British Ambassador in Constantinople in 1860's.[1]

It seems to this writer that the basic reasons for this failure discovered in the case of the Apostolic Church hold good for the Evangelicals, too. Therefore, the Armenian Protestant churches also need to reconsider and revise their approach and attitude to Islam. The following are *some* of the possible steps which could be taken by the Evangelicals, the writer being one of them:

(1) To amend the past failures, the *individualistic* experience of the Evangelicals should be broadened and supplemented by a *concern for others*, especially the Muslims. Although the Evangelicals *rightly* emphasized the experience of personal and individual salvation through faith in Christ, *they made it an end in itself*.[2] It was forgotten that we were "saved to serve." The Armenian Protestants followed the Calvinistic individualism and ignored their missionary task. Safety from future hell fire was considered sufficient.

(2) However genuinely spiritual were the motives of the Armenian Protestant forefathers, still, they too, were dominated by a nationalistic outlook, from a religious angle. The *name* they chose for the first church, persisting to our day, amply indicates this. It was Christened "The Evangelical Church of Armenia," in contrast with the "Holy Apostolic Church of Armenia." And there is ample ground to confess that *Armenia* was stressed as much as *Evangelical*.

The fire of evangelical faith was burning in the hearts of the early Protestant Armenians, but it was a zeal for *their own people*—the Armenians, and for Armenia. However praiseworthy, their quest for religious freedom was aimed at seeing the *Armenian Church* restored to its early evangelical purity. Here we must quote the leaders of the *forty*

---

[1] Anderson, *op. cit.*, II, 31.

[2] See S. Utujian, *Birth and Progress of Evangelicalism Among Armenians* (Armenian text); (Constantinople: Arax Press, 1914), pp. 160–162.

persons who organized the first Armenian Evangelical (Protestant) Church. When they were asked what name they would choose and to what denomination they would like to adhere, they answered:

> We do not need to decide on a new denomination or to adopt any foreign system fully. We are the disciples of the Holy Gospel and having already adopted its life-giving principles, we wish to restore our mother church to its original apostolic orthodoxy and simplicity; therefore, we have decided to be organized (as) Evangelical Church of Armenia, and nothing else.[1]

One cannot but admire the sincerity and courage of these thirty-seven men and three women who staked everything for their religious ideal. Yet, judging from all the subsequent history, it was a localized and national longing rather than a longing for the regeneration of Armenians *as well as non-Armenians.*

The story of Armenian life in Turkey *might* have been different *if* the Protestant pioneers had had the vision of calling the new church "The Evangelical Church of Christ" or "The Evangelical Church," and aimed at bringing into it every race, nation, and class.

Language would not have been a problem here, because Turkish and Armenian were used equally in these churches. In fact, we hear of some Turks attending services held in Turkish, and that there were about fifteen Turkish converts in Constantinople in 1864, the fruit of the endeavors of the missionaries of the American Board in Turkey.[2]

The real problem to be faced was: could a Turk or Arab or Kurd be a Christian and enter the Armenian Evangelical Church as a member while remaining a Turk or Arab? An elderly minister who is now deceased told this writer in person: "We wanted the Turks first to become Armenian;" that is, the implication was that to be a Christian meant to be identified with the Armenian people. Of course, no Turk would face *that.*

Therefore, as in the case of the Apostolic Church, so the Protestant Armenian Church should be "denationalized"—while preserving its genuinely spiritual motives. That means, it should recognize its supra-national nature and become the church for all who confess Christ—of whatever race, nationality, or culture.

(3) The Evangelical Church should revise its *dogmatic Biblicism.* The Bible—as in all Protestant Christendom—had replaced the ecclesiastical authority of the Armenian Apostolic Church. Therefore,

---

[1] S. Utujian, *op. cit.,* p. 167.

[2] Richter, *op .cit.,* pp. 173 ff.

the Armenian Prostetant stressed the binding authority of an *infallible Book*, rather than preaching a living Christ. This, naturally, would conflict with the Muslim idea of a divine *Quran* sent from heaven. And when the sword was wielded by those who accepted and followed an infallible and eternal *Quran*, and who were sworn to defend it, the conflict of *two infallible Books* would obstruct any Evangelical approach to Islam.

Therefore, the Protestant emphasis on an infallible *Book* should be abandoned in favor of an infallible and living Savior and a living experience of fellowship with the spirit, life, character, and teachings of Jesus Christ—whom Muslims respect, as repeatedly indicated before.

(4) The doctrinal position of the Protestant Armenians also should be rectified. The dogmatic approach of the Trinitarian formula and the *stress* upon the divinity of Christ have been used equally by the Evangelicals as by the Apostolic Armenians. Even though Protestants are affiliated with the Congregational fellowship, the Christology of the Evangelicals has been oriented toward Monophysitism.

To be sure, the birth, life, ministry, and death of Jesus Christ have been much dwelt upon—as they are by the Apostolic Armenians. But they have been *interpreted* in the same spirit as by the Apostolic Church.[1] The perfect divinity of Christ has been the center of attention. The Old Testament prophecies, the teachings, sinless life, miraculous birth, and miracles of Jesus have been adduced to *prove* his perfect Godhead rather than the perfect love of God for men. However much the humanity of Christ has been affirmed, his divinity has loomed large in the minds of those who have participated in any general discussion or ordination examination—the writer recalling his own ordination.[2]

Thus, if not in words, in psychological attitude the Monophysite Christology of the Apostolic Armenians has been adopted by the Evangelicals and the Incarnation remained a semi-real puzzle. Adding the Trinitarian formula to a non-realistic Christology, the Protestant Armenians also have been in want of an intellectual means of contact with Islam.

Consequently, the movement that made a right start and might have been the solution of the problem of the evangelization of Islam and, thereby, of Muslim-Armenian relations, came to the same tragic end.

---

[1] See *supra*, p. 126, *footnote 2*.

[2] When *many* questions were asked of him about the Deity of Christ; even about the *possibility* of repentance in the world to come; but *none* was asked as to the minister's responsibility for his non-Christian neighbors.

Even if a few Turkish or Arab Muslims had shown interest in hearing the Gospel, and even if a few had been actually baptized,[1] it had remained simply a casual interest, without any lasting effects.

When, therefore, Muslim-Turkish interests collided with the Armenian Apostolic Church and national aspirations, the Protestant Armenians were not differentiated; they, too, were liquidated and the remnants dispersed.

Obviously, therefore, the Armenian Evangelical Church, too, needs a reconsideration and revision of its doctrinal and Christological position. To evangelize Islam, it should begin where the Muslim world stands, namely, present the life and teachings of the Prophet Jesus the Messiah (*Isa-al-Masih*) and his matchless life of love and service, rather than starting with dogmatic, Trinitarian, approach, leaving to the wisdom of God and guidance of the Holy Spirit to help them comprehend, subsequently, the Divinity of Christ.

(5) Finally, as in the case of the Apostolic Armenians, so the Protestant Armenians should teach their constituents to distinguish between Islam and the Turks; organize to study the history of Muslim-Christian relations; appreciate and utilize the favorable passages of the *Quran* for Christians and Jesus; understand the claims, denials, and the misunderstandings of Islam and the *Quran* as to the Christian faith, the person of Christ, and the Christians in general;[2] organize study circles and young people's clubs where Muslims and Christians can come into contact and conduct friendly discussions; place the study of Islam and the *Quran* on the curricula of the Evangelical schools; preach Christian forgiveness of the enemies; organize philanthropic societies to serve and assist Muslims in poverty and distress; launch out a campaign of personal evangelism; work out a sound plan of Christian literature for Muslims, especially an intensive distribution of the Scriptures; and, recognizing the supra-national nature of the Christian Gospel and the Christian Church, present them to the Muslim world as historical realities through which *all men* everywhere are called into the fellowship of God's spirit as manifested in Jesus Christ.

In closing, what was stated about the Apostolic Church must be reiterated about the Protestant Armenian Church: It must reconsider its doctrinal theological stand and revise what needs revision; disengage itself from nationalistic tendencies and motives, while remaining loyal to the spirit of Christian patriotism; become the evangelical

---

[1] Addison, *op. cit.*, p, 65; Anderson, *op. cit.*, I, 379; II, 31–32.
[2] Addison, *op. cit.*, Chap. XVI, pp. 287., *passim*.

church for all who wish to join it, irrespective of nationality, race, and culture; shift from Biblicism to a Christo-centric emphasis, and present to the Muslim world a living Christ interpreted by the Gospel records of the human life of Jesus of Nazareth, whom Muslims recognize as a prophet of God—holding the doctrinal interpretation of his person for subsequent consideration.

In a word, God should be proclaimed to Islam as the Creator *as well as* the Father of all mankind; that He has spoken to humanity through His prophets—Moses, Jesus, Muhammad, and others; and that the *aim* of the Christian Church is to discover and follow the TRUTH, wherever it may be, whoever may have spoken it, wherever it may lead us.

EPILOGUE

The foregoing survey of the relevance of the Christology of the Armenian Church to its relations with the Muslim environment has been a painful task to the writer who loves his people and with whom he has tasted the gall of persecution, suffering, and massacre. But the facts of history must be faced in order to gather benefit from them.

Secular as well as ecclesiastical history testifies that Armenians belong to one of the oldest continuous branches of the human family of the Near East. As a nation, it has achieved a civilization and culture of its own. The geographical location of its homeland in an area where the three continents of Asia, Africa, and Europe converge, may explain much of its political vicissitudes as a people—trodden under the feet of the Empires of the East as well as the West. It has been endowed with great talents to build a strong nation and a prosperous country. It possessed "grit," industry, fortitude, courage, gallantry, loyalty to ideals, love of art, music, architecture, family fidelity, pride of race, vision of independent national existence, love of education, and willingness to die for its religious faith. These, however, were weakened by disunity, rivalry, and provincial individualism.[1]

These pages were written not to criticise its past, but to answer a question concerning its history. With such praiseworthy traits and possibilities and a long standing Christian faith, why did the Armenians fail to evangelize their Muslim environment? So much so, that it ended with their nearly complete extermination in their historic homeland in Asia Minor, where no Armenian churches or people are to be found today, excepting the remnant in Soviet Armenia. This dissertation was a modest attempt to answer this question by locating the *causa sui* of this failure.

To reiterate, risking tedium,[2] this thesis has maintained that the Monophysite Christology of the Armenian Church had a direct relevance to and bearing upon the relations of the Armenians with their Muslim environment. It was granted that *many* other factors have entered into the picture—geographical, political, racial, national, economic, international, and cultural. Our concern was with *one* of these, namely, the ecclesio-doctrinal position of the Armenian Church.

---

[1] Lynch, *op. cit.*, I, 255, 314, 391, 465–468.
[2] *Supra*, pp. 7 ff., 39 ff., 85 ff., 105 ff.

It has been demonstrated that the Monophysite Christology was the primary cause of the final rupture of the Armenian Church with the Church of the Empire—Eastern and Western—resulting in its condemnation as heretical and schismatic. This forced her to self-centered isolation, self-defense against the persecutions and encroachments of the orthodox churches, and to religious isolationism rather than aggressive expansion.[1]

The Monophysite Christology, by interpreting the Incarnation artificially and superficially—emphasizing the divinity at the expense of the perfectly human personality of Christ—led the Armenian Church to dogmatism, ceremonialism, sacramentarianism, sacerdotalism, iconolatry, and Mariolatry, *causing* the loss of the spiritual and moral vitality of the Christian faith and the consequent inability to attract or influence the Muslim environment.[2]

The unrealistic interpretation of the Incarnation and the overemphasis of the divine nature of Christ occasioned the neglect of the study, appeal, and application of the human life of Jesus of Nazareth. Thus, the Armenian Church and people denied themselves the opportunity of offering Christianity as a way of life, manifested through the human kindness, love, magnanimity, service, forgiveness, purity, self-sacrifice, and faith of Jesus. It ignored the complete dependence of Jesus on God as his Father, and his perfect love for men. It deprived the Armenians of the only practical and intelligible approach to Islam—namely, through the life and teachings of Jesus of Nazareth whom the Muslims honor as the son of Mary and one of God's prophets.[3]

Furthermore, the Monophysite Christology was employed as a barricade and embankment to protect the autonomy of the Armenian Church, while the Church constituted a shield and bulwark to protect the national identity of the Armenian people. Now Church and nation were identified, and the ecclesiastical autonomy of the Church and the political fortunes and survival of the nation completely engrossed the hearts and minds of the hierarchy of the Armenian Church. Naturally, the pre-occupation with the ecclesio-doctrinal independence and national survival barred the Church and people from perceiving the significance of the great opportunity and the importance of the urgent task of the evangelization of the Muslim neighbors.[4]

---

[1] *Supra*, chapter IV, pp. 62 ff.
[2] *Supra*, chapter IV, pp. 63 ff.
[3] *Supra*, chapter V, pp. 74 ff., 82ff.
[4] *Supra*, chapter II, pp. 37 ff.; VI, pp. 99 ff.

Moreover, the Christological divergence was used as a wall of partition to prevent the ecclesiastical and national assimilation of the Armenians with the Greeks. This religio-national self-isolation and severance from the Church of the majority obstructed cooperation with the Church of the Empire which was expanding by missionary endeavor both in the East and in the West,[1] whereas, closer fellowship with it might have strengthened the hands of the Armenians to undertake the task of the evangelization of the Near East as their share of the world responsibility of the Church Universal.

Again, over-emphasis of the Monophysitic definition of the divinity of Christ and the neglect of his completely human personality widened the intellectual and theological chasm between the Armenians and the Muslim world. To Islam, with its very simple creed,[2] the Trinity and the divine Sonship of Christ were incomprehensible—in fact, even profanity.[3]

Finally, the Armenian Church—protected by its Monophysitic segregation, and identified with the national aspirations of its people, acted as the guardian angel of Armenian national integrity; the hierarchy of the Church actively participated in national politics;[4] this completely blocked any intercourse between the Armenian Church and the Muslim state save formal relations; and the relations of the two faiths and peoples were further strained. The result was clash and destruction.

Thus, Christological isolation, national aspirations, and political conflicts—combined with ceremonialism, sacramentarianism, and sacerdotalism—appear to have extinguished the original missionary spirit and zeal of the Armenian Church. It had become a schismatic-dogmatic and isolated institution, identified with the nation, and serving as the citadel of Armenian national identity.[5] Therefore, when it confronted the Muslim faith and state, there had remained no missionary vitality or ambition to evangelize the adherents of this new religion. And when the national aspirations of the subject people—the Armenians—conflicted with those of the ruling nation—Muslim Arabs and Turks—the outcome was inevitably evil.

The political aspirations of the Armenians had put them under the ban of Muslim law fighting those who refused submission to Islam or

---

[1] Adeney, *op. cit.*, pp. 355 ff.; Walker, *op. cit.*, pp. 133 ff., 195 ff.

[2] Barton, *Christian Approach*, p. 51.

[3] Sweetman, *op. cit.*, I, 72–77; II, 89–114.

[4] See *supra*, page 108, *footnote* 1, and pp. 102, 103.

[5] Der-Nersessian, *op. cit.*, pp. 29–54.

to pay tribute as subjects; their religious faith was at variance and in enmity with the Muslim faith and its *Ulamas*; Christologically, they were isolated and alienated from the Western Christendom, too far in distance as well as sympathies to enjoy any protection; and nationally they were considered enemies of Turkish nationalism. Therefore, to massacre and destroy such a people would be rewarded—*sawab*—because, they seemed to be the political enemies of the land and the "accursed" opponents of the "true" faith of Islam.[1]

Thus, it appears that the Monophysite Christology of the Armenian Church, as the wall of partition, has preserved it intact as an autonomous and heretical institution. Persecutions for doctrinal non-conformity have forced it to complete identification with the national interests of its people. Concern for national survival and ecclesiastical independence has forced it to cling tenaciously to its distinctive Christology and to act as the bulwark of Armenian nationalism. And national aspirations have ended in tragedy.

Therefore, it is apparent that the Christology of the Armenian Church while preserving it as an autonomous and national institution, has also become a source of the weakness and tragedies of the Armenians in their relations with the Muslim environment.[2]

However, this does not mean the *end* of the Armenians. Like the Phoenix, they and their Church will rise over the ashes of their ruins—as they have done repeatedly in the past. But the lessons of history are warning roadsigns. The Armenian Church and its people need to break their shell of self-isolation and cooperate with the Universal Church. Otherwise, their future might be as precarious as their past.[3] To recognize where it is in error; to forgive where it has been wronged; to recover what it has lost; and to be a living, aggressive, witness to Christ—this is the challenging call of the hour. For, God has a providential purpose for them in the Near East. Massacred, dispossessed, and dispersed in every corner, they have learned to pay the supreme price of martyrdom for their ideals.

One step more remains to be taken: To serve as aggressive witnesses and evangelists among the Muslims of the Near East and become THE *missionary nation*. By God's grace this can and must be done. For, unless the Near East is won to the Gospel, we cannot enjoy a stable peace.

---

[1] Green, *op. cit.*, p. 467.

[2] Gwatkin and Whitney, *The Cambridge Medieval History*, Vol. IV, *The Eastern Roman Empire* (New York, 1923), pp. 153–182.

[3] Cf. *Supra*, Preface, and p. 119, note 1.

Have not many of the modern wars originated somewhere in the area of the Near East: the Balkan Wars (1912), World War I, and World War II as its continuation?

And what people on earth is better equipped to be the new "obedient servant of Jehovah" for the Muslims of the Near East than the martyred people of the martyred Church of Armenia, with stubborn loyalty to the Christian faith and the Church of Christ, "in spite of dungeon, fire, and sword?"

THE END

APPENDIX

DIAGRAMS ILLUSTRATING THE RELATIONS OF THE ARMENIAN CHURCH WITH THE CHURCH OF THE EMPIRE AND THE MUSLIM ENVIRONMENT

A. *ca.* 325 *A.D.*

This diagram represents the Church of the Empire *united* around the Council of Nicaea, where the Armenian Church also was represented; the Nicene Creed was adopted by Armenians the same year. At this time the Armenian Catholicos was ordained by the Bishop of Caesarea. Therefore, it was *not* an *independent* or *national* church.

Diagram A

B. *In ca.* 371 *A.D.*

This represents the Armenian Church in communion with the Church of the Empire, but *independent* of Caesarea. King Bab appointed a rival Catholicos whom Basil of Caesarea refused to consecrate. Bishop Anthimus of Tyana ordained him. Thereafter none was ordained by Caesarea. The Church of Armenia became *autocephalous* but in fellowship with the Church of the Empire.

Diagram B

C. *In ca.* 381 *A.D.*

The Armenian Church, now *independent* of Caesarea, was within the family of the Church of the Empire. It is *probable* that it was represented at the Second General Council. However, whether present or not, the Armenians *officially accepted and adopted* the Canons of the Council of Constantinople, thus keeping in close fellowship with the other members of the Church of the Empire.

Diagram C

D. *In ca.* 403–431 *A.D.*

Invention of the Armenian *alphabet fully nationalized* the Armenian Church. Yet, *independent and nationalized, it adopted the Canons of the Council of Ephesus.* Thus, the Armenian Church, *independent* (371) and *fully nationalized* (ca. 403), kept in full communion with the Ecumenical Church, so that Catholicos Isaac and Patriarch Proclius of Constantinople exchanged cordial letters in 435 A.D. in regard to the expulsion of the new heretics—Nestorians—now under the ban of the Church and Empire. Isaac called a special Synod to assure Proclius that no Nestorians were found in Armenia, and that if discovered they would be expelled.

Diagram D

E. *In ca.* 451 *A.D.*

This was the year of war against Persians who tried to reimpose Mazdaism on Christian Armenians. When the *Council of Chalcedon* was convened, the Catholicos and leaders were in chains in Persia. They had sent a delegation to Byzantium to ask for military assistance against the Persians, but the Emperor declined to help. We do not know whether the Armenians were invited to the Council of Chalcedon. Invited or not, their attendance was out of the question because of their war of survival with the Persians and the imprisonment of their leaders in the Persian capital.

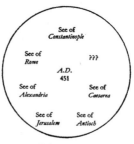

Diagram E

F. *In ca.* 490–506 *A.D.*
Peace was restored in 484–485 A.D. Papken I succeeded as Catholicos (490–516). Armenians first took notice of Chalcedon when some Persian "orthodox" Christians asked for advice against the "Nestorians" who were quoting the Chalcedonian decrees to defend their own views. Papken called a synod in Tevin (506 A.D.), which condemned Chalcedon as "Nestorian" and broke all relations with the Church of the Empire, declaring its allegiance to the first Three General Councils and affirming the one-nature formula. The *independent national* Church of Armenia turned *"schismatic."*

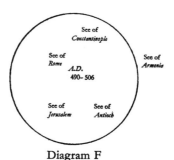

Diagram F

G. The break of the Armenian Church with the Church of the Empire on *doctrinal* grounds caused its complete self-isolation, persecution, identification with the nation, and *further and absolute* nationalization. Its *independence* began early, in the fourth century (371), but this did not cause a complete rupture with the Church Universal. It was *nationalized* early in the fifth century (ca. 403), but kept its communion with the Church of the majority. But *when it refused to recognize the doctrinal position of Chalcedon*, and insisted on the one-nature (Monophysite) formula of Cyril, it broke away completely (506) and was isolated.

Diagram G

H. Once the Armenian Church broke away and was self-isolated, it was persecuted as "heretical" and "schismatic." Already nationalized (ca. 403), persecutions forced the Church to *complete self-identification with the nation* and its interests. Now the Church clung to its Monophysitism to protect it from assimilation with the Greek Church, and in turn it (the Church) prevented the assimilation of the Armenian people by conserving the national heritage of the Armenians—language, literature, racial consciousness, customs, and traditions.

Diagram H

I. Now, Church and nation completely identified, whenever the Armenian Church was forced or coerced to yield its Monophysitic position and submit to the Byzantine or Roman Church, the Crown and the people, namely, the *nation*, as a body, stood by the Armenian Church and its hierarchy.

Or, when the Church and hierarchy tried to reach an understanding and agreement for reunion with the Church of the Empire, the Crown, the Princes, and the people—namely, the nation—along with dissident clergymen opposed and prevented the consummation of a reunion.

In every case, not the Armenian nationalism or the nationalized Church of Armenia, but the *Monophysitic dissent of the Church served as the wall of partition*, protecting the Church from assimilation; the Church protecting the *nation* from assimilation, and Church and nation assisting eachother in danger.

That *nationalism* was not a sufficient cause for break with the Church of the Empire is illustrated by the modern Russian Orthodox, Bulgarian Orthodox, Rumanian Orthodox, and the Greek Orthodox churches, none of which is any less nationalistic than the Armenian Church, but in full communion with one another because of their adherence to the Chalcedonian and the subsequent three Councils.

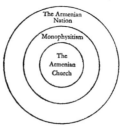

Diagram I

J. *In ca.* 640–1080 *A.D.*

When the Armenians came under the Muslim-Arab domination, the rôles of doctrine and nationalism—and many other factors—were inseparable in the life of the Armenian Church.

This diagram shows the fact that while the Armenian Church had already fully identified itself with the national life of its people, still, its doctrinal stand as to the *person of Christ* was *the* insurmountable religious and theological gap between the Muslim Arabs and the Armenians. For, the rule of Arabs was more politico-religious (theocratic) than nationalistic. It is only in recent times that Arab Muslims have awakened to what we call modern nationalism.

Therefore, in their subjection to the Muslim Arab rule, the Armenians would not have been—and were not—able to impress the ultra-unitarian mind of Islam by their Monophysitic approach to the person of Christ.

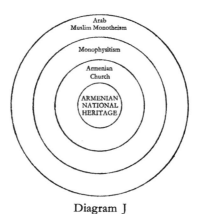

Diagram J

K. *In ca.* 1080–1915 *A.D.*

In its relations with the Turkish Empire, the position of the Armenian Church was similar to that under the Arab domination *until* the rise of modern nationalism among the Turks and Armenians.

At first, the religious stand of the Armenian Church would have made no appeal to the ultra-monotheistic mind of the Muslim Turks, *even if* they were willing and able to make any effort for the evangelization of Muslim Turks.

And when nationalistic conflicts strained the relations of the Armenians and the Turks, the Armenian Church was in no position to intervene and save the situation, because it had forgotten its missionary calling and become simply a nationalistic institution, being involved and often leading in national-political aspirations of Armenians.

This thesis attempted to delineate the development of these doctrinal-nationalistic-political events which ended in the tragedy of the Armenian Church and its people. The diagrams that preceded tried to illustrate *how* the *independent-national Church of Armenia* lived in fellowship with the Church of the Empire; how in 506 it broke away on *doctrinal* basis, and how this led to self-isolation, persecution, absolute nationalization, and calamity.

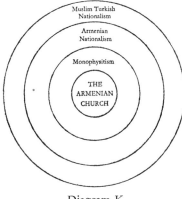

Diagram K

BIBLIOGRAPHY

I. *ARMENIA AND THE ARMENIAN CHURCH*

1. *General History*

A. Primary Sources—Armenian Text

Agathangelus, *History*. "Select Writers"; 3rd ed. Venice: St. Lazare Press, 1930.

Faustus of Byzantium, *History of the Armenians*. 4 parts. "Ancient Literature"; 4th ed. Venice: St. Lazare Press, 1933.

Lazare of Pharbe, *History of the Armenians and Epistle to Vahan Mamigonian*. "Select Writers"; 4th ed. Venice: St. Lazare Press, 1933.

Moses of Khorene, *History of the Armenians*. "Select Writers"; Venice: St. Lazare Press, 1881.

Yeghishe Vartabed (Elisaeus, doctor), *On Vartan and the War of the Armenians*. "Select Writers." Venice: St. Lazare Press, 1950.

B. Secondary Sources—Armenian Text

Der-Movsesian, S., *History of the Armenians: From the Beginning to Our Days*. Highest Course. 2nd ed. revised and completed. 2 vols. Venice: St. Lazare Press, 1922–1923.

Ormanian, M., *National History*: The Events of the Armenian Orthodox Church Narrated with the Related National Circumstances from the Beginning to Our Days. Vol. I, Constantinople: V. & H. Der-Nersessian, 1912; Vol. II, *From the Year 1221 to 1808, or from Constantine Partzrpertzi to Daniel Sourmaretzi*. Constantinople: V. & H. Der-Nersessian, 1914; Vol. III, *From 1808 to 1909: Post mortem* Publication Supervised by Archbishop P. Guleserian. Jerusalem: St. James Press, 1927.

C. Sources in Foreign Languages

Ananikian, M. H., "Armenia (Zoroastrian)," *Encyclopedia of Religion and Ethics*. Edited by James Hastings. Vol. I, 1922.

Arpee, L., *The Armenian Awakening: A History of the Armenian Church, 1820–1860*. Chicago: The University Press, 1909.

——, *A History of Armenian Christianity from the Beginning to Our Time*: A Centennial Volume Marking the One Hundredth Anniversary of Armenian Protestantism, 1846–1946. New York: The Armenian Missionary Association of America, Inc., 1946.

Brockelmann, C. *et al.*, *Geschichte der christlichen Litteraturen des Orients*. Zweite Ausgabe mit Berichtigungen. Leipzig: C. F. Amelangs Verlag, 1909, pp. 75–130.

Conybeare, F. C., *The Key of Truth*. Oxford: University Press, 1898.

Der-Nersessian, S., *Armenia and the Byzantine Empire: A Brief Study of Armenian Art and Civilization*. Preface by Henri Gregoire. Cambridge: Harvard University Press, 1945.

Encyclopedia Britannica. 14th ed. Vol. XIII. Article "Khazars."

——., Vol. XXII. Article "Van."

Finck, F. N., "Geschichte der armenischen Litteratur," *Geschichte der christlichen Litteraturen des Orients*. Edited by C. Brockelmann *et al*. 2nd ed. with corrections. Leipzig: C. F. Amelangs Verlag, 1909; 75–130.

Green, F. D., *Armenian Massacres or the Sword of Mohammed*. Containing a Complete and Thrilling Account of the Terrible Atrocities and Wholesale Murders Committed in Armenia by Mohammedan Fanatics, Including a Full Account of the Turkish People, Their History, Government, Manners, Customs, and Strange Religious Belief. To which is Added the Mohammedan Reign of Terror in Armenia. Edited by H. D. Northrop. Illustrated. Philadelphia: International Publishing Co., 1896.

Langlois, V., *Collection des Historiens anciens et modernes de l' Arménie*. 2 vols. Paris: Z. Renan, 1867–1869.

Lehmann-Haupt, C. F., "Urartu," *Encyclopedia Britannica*. Edited by J. L. Garvin. 14th ed. Vol. XXII, 1930.

Lynch, H. F. B., Armenia: *Travels and Studies*. In Two Volumes, with 197 Illustrations, Reproduced from Photographs and Sketches by the Author, Numerous Maps and Plans, a Bibliography, and a Map of Armenia and Adjacent Countries. Vol. I, *The Russian Provinces*; Vol. II, *The Turkish Provinces*. London: Longmans, Green, and Co., 1901.

Macler, F., "Armenia (Christian)," *Encyclopedia of Religion and Ethics*. Edited by J. Hastings. Vol. I, 1922.

Safrastian, A., "Armenia," *Encyclopedia Britannica*. Edited by J. L. Garvin. 14th ed. Vol. II, 1930.

Sayce, A. H., "Armenia (Vannic)," *Encyclopedia of Religion and Ethics*. Edited by J. Hastings. Vol. I, 1922.

Smith, E., *Researches of the Rev. E. Smith and Rev. H. G. O. Dwight in Armenia: Including a Journey Through Asia Minor, and into Georgia and Persia, with a Visit to the Nestorian and Chaldean Christians of Oormiah and Salmas*. In Two Volumes. Vol. II. Boston: Crocker and Brewster, 1833.

D. Modern Times

Gabrielian, M. C., *Armenia: A Martyr Nation*. New York: Fleming H. Revell Co. 1918.

Toynbee, A., *The Treatment of Armenians in the Ottoman Empire, 1915–16. Documents Presented to Viscount Grey of Fallodon, Secretary of State for Foreign Affairs, by Viscount Bryce. With a Preface by Viscount Bryce*. London: Sir Joseph Causton and Sons, Limited, 1916.

Vertanes, C., *Armenia Reborn*. New York: The Armenian National Council, 1947.

2. History of the Armenian Church

A. Primary Sources—Armenian Text. See page 142, A

B. Secondary Sources—Armenian Text

Guleserian, P., *The Church of the Armenians*. Studies on Problems Concerning the Reformation of the Armenian Church; The Position of the Armenian Church within the Universal Christian Church; Apostolicity of the Armenian Church; State and Church. Reprinted from "Zion" Magazine. Jerusalem: St. James Press, 1930.

Hatzooni, V., *Important Problems from the History of the Armenian Church*. Venice: St. Lazare Press, 1927.

Kassouny, Y. S., *The Missionary Spirit in the Armenian Church*. Aleppo: Bozoklian Press, 1940.
——, *The Path of Light: History of the Armenian Evangelical Movement, 1846–1946*. Beirut: The Armenian Missionary Association of America, Inc., 1947.
Ormanian, M., *The Church of the Armenians*. Its History, Doctrine, Government, Reformation, Ceremony, Literature, and Present Condition. 3rd ed. Reexamined. Constantinople: V. & H. Der-Nersessian, 1913.

C. Sources in Foreign Languages. See page 142, C

3. *Armenian Doctrine*

A. Primary Sources—Armenian Text

Agathangelus, See above, p. 142, A.
The Divine Liturgy According to the Rites of the Holy Apostolic Church of Armenians. Edited by A. Torossian, New York: The Gotchnag Press, 1933.
Gregory of Datev, *Book of Questions*. Constantinople, 1729.
Krikor Makistros., *Versification of Krikor Makistros of Bahlav*. Venice: St. Lazare Press, 1868.

B. Secondary Sources—Armenian Text. See above, p. 142, B.

Ormanian, M., *National History*. See page 142, B.

C. Sources in Foreign Languages

Conybeare, F. C., – See above, page 142, C.
The Divine Liturgy, According to the Rites of the Holy Apostolic Church of Armenians. Translated by A. Torossian. New York: The Gotchnag Press, 1933.
John of Otzun, *Tractate Against the Phantasiastae*. Translated by L. Arpee: *A History of Armenian Christianity*. New York: The Armenian Missionary Association of America, Inc., 1946, Appendix II, pp. 325–354.
Poladian, T., "An Armenian Reply to the Pope," *The Christian Century*, LVIII (December, 1951), pp. 1513–14.
Tiran, Bishop, *The Doctrinal Position of the Armenian Church*. A Paper by His Grace Bishop Tiran (at that time Vardapet), read before a circle of Anglican Theologians in Oxford, England, in the summer of 1943. New York: Diocese of the Armenian Church, 1947.

II. *SOURCES ON ISLAM*

1. *General History*

A. Primary Sources—Translations

Al-Ashari, Abu-'l-Hasan Ali Ibn-Ismail, *Kitab al Ibanah an Usul ad Diyana* (The Elucidation of Islam's Foundation). Translated by W. C. Klein. New Haven: American Oriental Society, 1940.
Al-Baghdadi, Abu-Mansour abd-al-kahir ibn-Tahir, *Al-Fark Bain al-Firak* (*Moslem Schisms and Sects*).2 vols.Vol. I, translated by K. C. Seelye. New York: Columbia University Press, 1919; Vol. II, translated by A. S. Halkin, Tel-Aviv, 1935.
Al-Ghazali, Abu-Hamid Muhammad ibn-Muhammad ibn-Ahmad, *Ar Radd al Jamil li Ilahiat Isa bi Sarih al Injil* (*Réfutation Excellente de la Divinité de Jésus-Christ d'Après les Evangiles*—Excellent Refutation of the Divinity of Jesus

Christ According to the Gospels). Translated by R. Chidiac. Paris: Librairie Ernest Leroux, 1939.

Holy Qur-an, The. Translated by M. Ali. Woking: The Islamic Review Office, 1917.

Al-Kindy, The Apology of Abd al-Masih ibn-Ishac al-Kindy. Translated by Sir W. Muir. London: Smith, Elder, & Co., 1882.

Koran, The. Translated from the Arabic by the Rev. J. M. Rodwell, M. A. Everyman ed. 6th Printing. London: J. M. Dent & Sons, Ltd., 1918.

Tabari, Ali, *Kitab ud Din wa Daula (The Book of Religion and Empire).* A Semi-Official Defence and Exposition of Islam Written by Order at the Court and with the Assistance of the Caliph Mutawakkil (A.D. 847–861). Translated with a Critical Apparatus from an Apparently Unique MS. in the John Rylands Library by A. Mingana, D.D. Manchester: At the University Press, 1922.

Al-Taftazani, Sa'd al-Din, *A Commentary on the Creed of Islam.* Sa'd al-Din al-Taftazani on the Creed of Najm al-Din al-Nasafi. Translated with Introduction and notes by E. E. Elder. New York: Columbia University Press, 1950.

B. Secondary Sources

Clark, E. L., *The Arabs and the Turks.* Their Origin and History, Their Religion, Their Imperial Greatness in the Past, and Their Condition at the Present Time, with Chapters on the Other Non-Christian Tribes of Western Asia. Boston: Congregational Publishing Society, 1876.

Dictionary of Islam, A. 2nd ed. 1935. Articles, "Abu-Hanifah," "Al-Ghazzali," "Jizyah," "Khalifah," (Caliph) "Muhammad," "Muhammadanism," "Mulla," "Quran," "Sects of Islam," "Shaikh," "Sufi," "Ulama," "Zimmah," and "Zimmi."

Faris, N. A. (ed.), *The Arab Heritage.* Princeton: Princeton University Press, 1944.

Hurgronje, C. S., *Mohammedanism.* Lectures on Its Origin, Its Religious and Political Growth, and Its Present State. "American Lectures on the History of Religions, Series of 1914–1915"; New York: G. P. Putnam's Sons, 1916.

Johnson, P. E., "Koran or Quran", *An Encyclopedia of Religion.* Edited by V. Ferm, 1945.

Macdonald, D. B., *Development of Muslim Theology, Jurisprudence, and Constitutional Theory.* "The Semitic Series"; New York: Charles Scribner's Sons, 1903.

Mingana, A., "Quran," *Encyclopedia of Religion and Ethics.* Edited by J. Hastings. Vol. X, 1924.

Morrison, P. G., "Algazali; Al-Ghazzali," *An Encyclopedia of Religion.* Edited by V. Ferm. 1945.

Smith, M., *Readings from the Mystics of Islam.* Translations from the Arabic and Persian, Together with a Short Account of the History and Doctrines of Sufism and Brief Biographical Notes on Each Sufi Writer. London: Luzac & Company Ltd., 1950.

Tritton, A. S., *The Caliphs and Their Non-Muslim Subjects.* Oxford, 1930.

Zwemer, S. M., *Islam, A Challenge to Faith.* New York: Laymen's Missionary Movement, 1907; Copyright, Student Volunteer Movement, New York, 1907.

2. Muslim Doctrine

A. Primary Sources—Translations

Al-Ashari – See above, page 144, II.

"Catechism of Abu-Hafs Umar al-Nafasi," translated by A. J. Wensinck, in *The Muslim Creed.* Its Genesis and Historical Development. Cambridge: At the University Press, 1932, pp. 263–264.

"The Fikh Akbar I," translated by A. J. Wensinck: *The Muslim Creed*. Cambridge, 1932, pp. 103–104.

"The Fikh Akbar II," tr. by A. J. Wensinck: *The Muslim Creed*. Cambridge: 1932, pp. 188–197.

Al-Ghazali, – See above, page 144, II.

Koran, The. – See above, page 145.

Al-Taftazani, – See above, page 145.

"The Wasiyat Abi Hanifa," translated by A. J. Wensinck: *The Muslim Creed*. Cambridge, 1932, pp. 125–131.

B. Secondary Sources

Ali, M., *The Religion of Islam*. Lahore: The Ahmadiyya Anjuman Inshaat Islam, 1936,

Ali, N., *Some Religious and Moral Teachings of Al-Ghazzali*. Freely rendered into English by Syed N. Ali. Baroda: The Seminar, The College, 1920.

A Dictionary of Islam. 2nd ed. 1935. Articles, "Creed," "God," "Heaven," "Hell," "Holy Spirit," "IJma," "Jesus Christ," "Paradise," "Pardon," "Predestination," "Qalam (Pen)", "Qiyas," "Repentance," "Ruah, Ruh," "Salvation," "Sin," "Soul," "Spirit," "Tables of the Law."

Encyclopedia of Islam: *A Dictionary of the Geography, Ethnography, and Biography of the Muhammadan Peoples*; *Prepared by a Number of Leading Orientalists*. Edited by M. Th. Houtsma et al. 4 vols. Leyden: E. J. Brill, Ltd., 1913–1934.

Ferm V., "Soul," *An Encyclopedia of Religion*. Edited by V. Ferm, 1945.

Guillaume, A., *The Traditions of Islam, An Introduction to the Study of the Hadith Literature*. Oxford: The Clarendon Press, 1924.

Johnson, P. E., "Koran or Quran," *An Encyclopedia of Religion*. Edited by V. Ferm. 1945.

Klein, F. A., *The Religion of Islam*. London: Kegan Paul, Trench, Trubner & Co., Ltd. 1906.

Macdonald, D. B., *Aspects of Islam*. New York: The Macmillan Company, 1911.

——, *Development of Muslim Theology, Jurisprudence, and Constitutional Theory*. "The Semitic Series"; New York: Charles Scribner's Sons, 1903.

Parrish, F. L., "Ruah," *An Encyclopedia of Religion*. Edited by V. Ferm. 1945.

Sell, E., "Sin (Muslim)," *Encyclopedia of Religion and Ethics*. Edited by J. Hastings. Vol. XI, 1924.

Smith, M., *Readings from the Mystics of Islam*. See above p. 145, B.

Sweetman, J. W., *Islam and Christian Theology*. A Study of the Interpretation of Theological Ideas in the Two Religions. In Three Parts. I, Origins (two volumes); II, Scholastic Development; III, Critical Reconstruction. Part One, Vol. I, *Preparatory Historical Survey of the Early Period*; Vol. II, *The Theological Position at the Close of the Period of Christian Ascendancy in the Near East*. "Lutterworth Library, Vol. XIX, Missionary Research Series, No. 6"; and "Vol. XX, No. 7"; London: Lutterworth Press, 1945–1947.

Thomson, W., "Al-Ashari and His Al-Ibanah." A Discussion and Critique of Walter C. Klein's Translation of *Al-Ashari's Al-Ibanah an usul-ad-diyanah* (American Oriental Series, vol. 19), American Oriental Society, New Haven, Connecticut, 1940. $ 2.00; *The Moslem World*. A Christian Quarterly Review of Current Events, Literature, and Thought among Mohammedans. XXXII (July, 1942), 242–260.

Tritton, A. S., *Islam: Belief and Practices*. New York: Hutchinson's University Library, 1951.